Backseat Inklings

Driving positivity into the world one rider at a time.

by

Donald Bouton

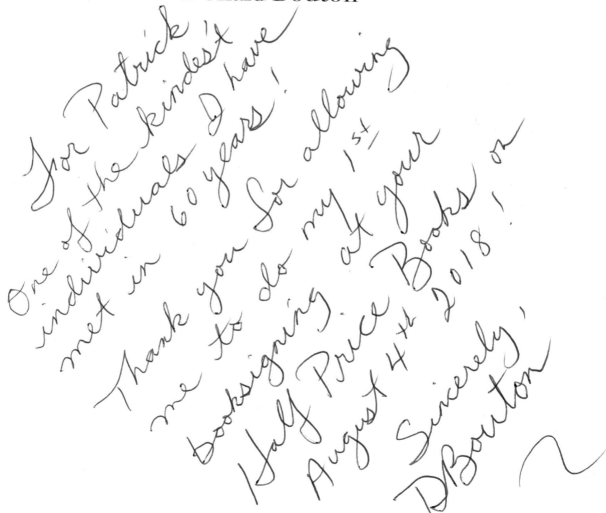

For Patrick!
One of the kindest
individuals I have
met in 60 years!
Thank you for allowing
me to do my 1st
booksigning at your
Half Price Books on
August 4th 2018!
Sincerely,
DBouton

For additional copies please contact Create Space at www.createspace.com

Published by Donald Bouton with CreateSpace.

ISBN 0692787453
CreateSpace Title ID 6600012

Edited by David L. Mosser and Andrew Twenter.

Special appreciation to all the riders and writers.

I wish to dedicate "Backseat Inklings" to my best friend and beautiful wife of thirty-four years.

I remember first meeting her in the Towers cafeteria at Southeast Missouri State University in Cape Girardeau, Missouri where she was working hard to keep guys like me from eating more than once. The way she didn't take any junk from all of the guys made me realize that I really liked how spunky she was. To this day she is as spunky as ever.

After buying two tickets to see the band Starcastle over at the "Hush Puppy" on the east side of the Mississippi, I finally got the courage to ask her out on a date…at least I thought I asked her out! I guess when I went up to her to ask her out I said, "I have some tickets" instead of saying I have two. When I drove up to her dorm she came up to the car and said, "Where's everyone else?" I didn't know what to say, but thank goodness she decided to hop in and still go with me!

I actually think after our first date on October 9th, 1979 I knew I was going to ask her to marry me! Our conversation flowed and it seemed like time was standing still. I was mesmerized by her blond hair and sparkling blue eyes.

She has definitely turned my life around for the better. I shudder to imagine what my life would be like without her!

I Love You so much Trish!

Forward by Marcus Engel

Isn't technology amazing? I'm always a fan of a company that can, as the ancients used to say, build a better mousetrap. We're living in the most technologically advanced era of all time. That is, until 10 minutes from the time you read this. Then, technology will prove itself to be bigger, better, faster and stronger.

All of humanity benefits from technological advancements. For those of us with disabilities, that's even more true. I've played both sides of the fence. At 18, I lost my sight (and almost my life) in a motor vehicle crash caused by a second party drunk driver. One minute I was riding home with friends after a St. Louis Blues hockey game, the next I was laying in an intersection with every bone in my face crushed. The blindness was total, instantaneous and permanent...that is, until someone in biomedical sciences comes up with an alternative to sight. What that will look like, no one knows right now. Personally, I'm not holding my breath.

While there were, of course, adaptations to be made, I was fortunate that technology existed that would lessen the diminishing effects of blindness. In the 20+ years since that night, the playing field has continually been leveled with technology that makes life much, much more accessible to blind folks like me.

I'm fond of saying that Uber is the second best invention ever for people who are blind or visually impaired. It is only outranked by the smartphone on which to use the Uber app. Now, though I haven't been able to drive for decades, I can whip out my smart phone, swipe and flip through a few icons and, next thing I know, a car pulls up to take me wherever I want to go. That's something I couldn't have imagined in my wildest dreams, even as recently as five or six years ago. Now? It's one of my primary modes of transportation.

Such it was on the night when an Uber pulled up at my hotel. It was then that I met Don. Being blind, there's always a bit of hesitation getting into a car with someone you've never met before. Will this driver break the law and not allow me in because of my Seeing Eye dog? Any possibility this driver may rob me of my money and push me out of the car in an abandoned area? Not likely...but still possible.

Once inside Don's car, any of those irrational fears melted away. I'm a total extrovert, so I almost always strike up a conversation with my drivers. Same thing with Don. I found him to be a competent, compassionate individual who is driven by service to others. Plus, he's just a nice guy!

Don explained that he'd been keeping a notebook of his riders. It was more than a superficial resume of those who've ridden in his vehicle, but rather, Don used his intellect and perception to go a little deeper, interviewing riders as to what motivates them. He asked if there was a certain quote or life philosophy that has guided me during struggles. I didn't have to think about this. Immediately, that little bit of knowledge sprung to mind: a lyric by the Nobel Prize winning poet, Bob Dylan.

See, as I lay clinging to life in a hospital bed just a few miles from where Don picked me up, I experienced what is, I think, one of the worst things a human being could ever endure. The permanent disability of blindness was, strangely enough, not as hard to deal with as the physical trauma. With a dislocated right hip and a broken left leg, I was completely immobile. With jaws wired shut, I could not eat or drink. Because of the trach in my throat, I could not speak. Without sight, I could not distract myself from the pain. And, oh God, the pain. It was immense and never ending.

Once it was established that I would probably live, I made the commitment to return to college ASAP. Little did I know how long the physical recovery would take nor the challenges I would meet along the way. But, lying in the hospital bed, roughly void of several of my senses, I took inspiration from Bob Dylan. Music was, and always will be, the art I enjoy most. And because I'm a reader and a writer, lyric and verse speak loudly to me. Sometime in the early dawn hours, a head full of insomnia and a face full of horrific pain, Bob Dylan's "Just Like Tom Thumb's Blues" came on the stereo.

Please know, I'd owned Dylan's Greatest Hits Volume II for several years prior. I loved every song on this double album and knew every word by heart. Yet that night in that hospital bed, the second line of the song was highlighted, underlined and shouted into my soul: "Negativity don't pull ya through…"

From that moment, Dylan's words became my mantra. I knew that I couldn't focus on all the horrible things that had happened to me. Rather, I needed to focus on the positive things I still had; my friends, my family and my brain. How I crushed every bone in my face and walked away with no traumatic brain injury is a miracle in and of itself.

"Negativity don't pull ya through", I said to Don. "It's a line from a Bob Dylan song and it's the reason I'm alive." I went on to explain how, in the years of recovery and adaptation post trauma, those words kept me motivated, kept me positive and kept me sane. They are as true to me as anything written by Plato, Shakespeare or Homer.

When Don shared his vision for this project, I had to smile. Pulling the collective knowledge of the common man (or Uber rider) is another way to help heal the hurts in our world. When we learn the stories of others, when we sit without judgement as stories are shared and then those pearls of wisdom are shared, we begin to see human compassion emerge as the driving force of all things in the universe. Thank you, Don, for having the insight to gather these stories, quotes and bits of wisdom that will certainly help to heal humanity, one rider (or reader!) at a time.

Introduction by the Author

Before you turn the pages and begin to read the inspirational entries that fill this journal, allow me to explain how it all started. You see, I've been an Uber Driver since November 2015. I have over 2,200 trips under my belt and still find it to be exhilarating, fascinating, and adventurous! I enjoy the anticipation of who may be my next rider and where their destination will be.

My main motivation for Uber driving is to keep the members of our community safe from the poor judgement of people who drive under the influence of alcohol or other drugs. Recently, a close family friend was the victim of a motor-vehicle accident caused by a by a highly intoxicated young driver trying to evade law enforcement. All who know her are grateful for her remarkable recovery. It was inspiring to watch her fight to recover just in time to walk down the aisle in her daughter's wedding!

In April of 2016, after driving for six months I decided to spice things up a bit. I started asking my riders to jot down a thought, quote, or a motivating force on a yellow note pad that just happened to be on my backseat. About a week later, what I saw was a mishmash of random thoughts with no real direction. Then a young man used his Uber App to signal for a ride. I was fortunate to be the closest driver to the Frontenac Hilton Hotel where he was staying. Upon pulling up to the hotel, a young well-dressed man by the name of Marcus Engel entered the backseat of my midnight blue Acura TSX along with his best friend Garrett. Garrett happens to be a handsome Yellow Labrador Retriever as well as this gentleman's service dog. I vividly recall moving the front passenger seat as far forward as it would go so Garrett could sit at attention at the feet of his master because, of course, he was still on duty. Thus far Garrett is the only service dog I have had the pleasure of driving!

The 18 minute ride went by quickly because Marcus and I had a terrific conversation about an assortment of topics. Marcus shared how he lost his sight at the young age of eighteen in an automobile accident caused by an intoxicated person driving the other car. After the accident and the emotional trauma of learning he would be blind the rest of his life, he then focused on overcoming the physical damage to his body. Hard work along with hours of physical therapy and occupational therapy has indeed been worth it! It's allowed him to travel the world sharing his inspirational story of overcoming adversity.

Prior to arriving at his destination I asked Marcus to share what has helped him get through the tough times. Without hesitation he asked me to jot down "Negativity Don't Pull Yah Through", a lyric from one of Bob Dylan's classics, "Just Like Tom Thumb's Blues".

Immediately after Marcus and Garrett got out of my car I began asking my riders "What is the most positive force in your life?" To my surprise, nearly everyone jumped at the chance to jot down their unique stories, along with their first name and where they are from. Passengers were obviously intrigued by other riders' entries and frequently pushed me to share these personal and inspirational stories with the rest of the world. I even had several riders ask me to keep driving so that they could read more of the other entries. It's the encouragement from riders, family, and friends that has driven me to share this journal with the world.

Thank you Marcus for inspiring me to start asking my riders to share their positive stories and on top of that, agreeing to write the foreword! I hope those of you who are reading this check out Marcus' many works on his website: www.marcusengel.com.

Now to explain the title; Backseat Inklings. Giving this journal a name proved to be challenging. But one night while my wife and I were watching a rerun of Friends, she suddenly shouted, "I know what to call it...Backseat Inklings!" It was perfect! You may understand the Backseat part, but the Inklings half is derived from my mother's poetry book she penned over fifty years ago! Her poetry collection is entitled, "Inklings" because she wrote with a quill she dipped into an inkwell her father used at his desk serving as Principal of Shaw School in St. Louis in the early 1900's. Mom lined the top of her roll-top desk with her treasured collection of inkwells and feather quills. Now I treasure all twenty-three of them!

Since I asked my riders to write down a positive force in each of their lives, I hope you don't mind me sharing a bit about some of the positive forces in my life.

My mother's amazing display of faith in Christ. It was this faith that helped her endure the loss of three of her six children to depression. She was patient, kind, and nurturing to all. She was a helper and healer at heart, thus her job as an occupational therapist suited her well. On top of all that she was my wonderful Mom who I love and miss dearly!

My father was a positive force. He taught me numerous lessons I continue to use in my day to day life. He wanted me to trust people, but not have blind trust.

He stressed that people are generally good and mean well, but each has a bias or prejudice whether realizing it or not. I did not know how smart he was until I became a father; funny how that works, huh? I can only hope my children will think that about me one day.

My "other Mother" must be included in my list of positive forces. My mother in law was an amazing woman! After losing her husband at way too early of an age, she stayed strong for her children, grandchildren, and great grandchildren. She quietly led by example...going back to school in her 60's to become a chaplain. She devoted hours of her time to her church. Then showed great bravery in the way she battled cancer until she died the way she wanted...in her own home. No one recalls hearing her complain during her battle. On top of all that she was a great listener and supported me during my personal struggles.

My thirty year old son inspires me by how passionate he is about working as a physical therapist helping others to alleviate pain and optimize their function in their daily lives. He is grateful that several outstanding physical therapists were able to significantly help in his recovery after being stricken with an autoimmune muscle disease. The positive impact of many physical therapy sessions greatly influenced his decision to become a doctor of physical therapy. He now helps his patients overcome their pain and limitations associated with disease, injury, or dysfunction of the body. I am so very proud to be able to call him "son"!

My twenty-five year old kind -hearted daughter inspires me by how she demonstrates bravery and courage in unexpected situations. She always knows what to say to brighten my day! She has found her passion in occupational therapy after suffering a crushing injury to her hand and received excellent care from a kind occupational therapist. I'm certain she will prove to be a wonderful OT like her grandmother.

Next to Jesus, the most positive force in my life is hands down my wife. She continues to show me her love each and every day and keeping her "for better or worse" wedding vow even after me testing her over and over. She has been the love of my life, the rock of our family, and an amazing mother to our two children. I admire her tenacious work ethic working long and hard hours for her family and a hospital devoted to saving the lives of children. I love you sweetheart!

Really, who would have thought me picking up a guy and his dog could lead to something so cool and unique? My riders, or should I call them my writers, have openly shared their stories. Many of these stories are about overcoming adversity, receiving loving advice from Mom, Dad, Grandma, Grandpa, a special teacher, or a comforting caregiver, nurse or friend.

From April of 2016 to October 2016 I enjoyed having conversations with people from thirty-seven different countries, coincidently thirty-seven different states, plus one person from Puerto Rico. Speaking with them and reading their uplifting entries renews my belief that people are good hearted and basically want the same things in life; freedom, happiness, openly practicing their choice of faith, publicly voicing their opinions, raising a family, and showing love for one another.

Now that I have been given the chance to push the reset button, I believe God is not done with me yet and expects much more out of me. I have wondered myself if this journal could be part of His plan for keeping me around.

To My Riders: I can't thank you enough for encouraging me to share these inklings and making this happen! See you on the road again soon!

I sincerely hope you enjoy reading "Backseat Inklings" as much as I have!

May God Bless you and your loved ones!

Sincerely,

Donald N. Bouton

Volume I

4/6/16 "Negativity Don't Pull you through!"

From Bob Dylan

— GARRETT MY SERVICE DOG

& MarcusEngel.com
Motivational Speaker
From St. Louis, Mo

Rockwld Teacher Be polite be humble be proactive be accountable!

Trump 2016 anti-est. bi-anti-establishment! Love him!

Enjoy the ride!

ERIC
SE
Construction
Manager

EAT THE ELEPHANT ONE BITE AT A TIME,
AND LAUGH ALONG THE WAY

Work hard, play hard
 - Bowen   WashU '17

Rita
(China)
WashU

Spend more time on exploring my
life, my surroundings, and this
wonderful world. Just don't
spend so much time on doing
MATH :)

Kristen
SLU

Go outside and adventure
more. The world is a beautiful
place. Don't stress to much,
it wont matter as much as you
think it will.

2

Tip at least 20%
(a waiter from Kirkwood, Mo)

Jim From Ja Basel

Go on a trip. Have ~~a drink~~ a drink. Try something new.

Reine It is what it is!

MK Don't be a dumbass.

4/7/16   Austin;
Real Estate Developer;
My brain is too fried
to think right now!

3

4/7/16

~~Nothing good~~ Art is a
cross between witnessing
and creating. Yes, you are
doing the physical production,
but it is the unplanable that
eventually drives the work.
If you know what it is going
to look like before you start making
it, you are not creating, you
are executing.
— Jack,
WUSTL
student

The journey is the reward.
Jason, California

Always assume good intentions.
Everyone you meet has a story
to tell, or may be fighting a
battle you know nothing about.
Lucy, CA.

4

Allison: Persistence is key.
Always keep trying

Tin: God first, Others second,
Self last

M: Let's Go Blues

Jessica
From
Columbia
IL
watched the cards game!
Amazing!! Then called
my ~~parents~~ Uber and
had the best, safe ride
home.

John
. (Jesus)
He must become greater
and I must become
lesser

the past is history, the
future is mystery,
and today a is a gift.
That is why we call it
present. - written by
(a 9yr.old) Matthew CA
               - From kung fu
               ~~no~~ panda turtle
               old guy

To thine own self be true
for as night follows day
thou cannot be false to any
man
                              Marvin 5th
                              Hamlet I ~~III~~

CARPE DIEM

               - UNKNOWN

6

Marlo

riders in the storm —
Bring your umbrella!
Manton, California

Sarah

Put a bird on it.
— Portland, OR

Rebecca

If it doesn't matter
In the scope of eternity,
Let it Go!
— Dayton, OH

Derek
Los Angeles

"Candy is dandy but liquor is quicker."

— Willy Wonka

Katherine

~Pittsburgh, PA

You never know how strong you really are until you have to. The toughest times can reap the greatest rewards

Jason the Red Nose Wrestler

St.Louis

Happiness is only real when shared.

Katie C

Work U

Pt guard

I can do all things through Christ who strengthens me

Phil. 4:13

ellen w.

Birmingham

I would rather have done it & regretted it than not have done it at all.

8

The future is now. All you
have is the moment. Step into
it with your whole heart.
—Chelsea

4.8.16

Happiness comes from
within; get in touch
with it and never have
a grey day in your life
again.
— Vitoria
Brazil
4/8/16

"Be certain that you do
not die without having
done something wonderful
for humanity" — Maya Angelou

Deja
4/8/16
STL

Be happy! :) Amanda
- STL

9

Dear Diary,
I'm 28 today! Is my
lyf where it needs to be?!

Brittany
R. 16
4/8/16

Life is great! Don't use do
something stupid!

Arjun
St. Lous

"Be humble or get humbled"

Phillip
P.
St. Louis

Contribute to this world.
-Chloe - St. louis, MO

10

Robin

Insightful with the journey that God has graced me with.

Steve

Be nice to the world make it a better place to live in.

Live in the ~~moment~~ no

regrets, be kind to

everyone... you don't know their story.

Say I love you to someone every day, hug often, kiss often

11

Angela Love - I love being with
friends who are so fun and we
reminese about previous times.
Wash, MO

Scott Miller the Philosopher -
my msg to the world is peace, love
and chill out! Its all good. Wash, MO

Nate Pardy - Clarity is important,
in everyday life. Lets fix this!
SH

Jill - Be true to you.
Whoever that if - Dont conform!
Wash, MO

Give thanks for wonderful friends!

When - list color of car -
of driver -
great weide -
love it in STL.

12

Lundi 11 Avril 2016

Sur cette victoire 10-1 des Cardinals par aux Brewers, je me rend au bureau Mon conseil pour que ce soit en bront ces quelques mots. Il s'agit de faire preuve d'empathie et de s'élever de sa condition tout en restant authentique et humble.

"Ce que tu as hérité de tes pères, acquiers le pour le posséder"... et assimile le pour le transmettre aux générations qui suivront.

Forget your partner - get, bh -
remember your family. They will never
betray, they will always have your back,
Just when you think you are lowest
you will be of your highest priority
friendship.
    Uber is savior

"IF YOUR DOG IS TOO FAT, YOU NEED MORE
   EXCERCISE OR QUIT TAKING UBER..... NOT!
I LOVE UBER AND ALL THE DRIVERS
THAT ARE INVOLVED.
        J.D. "
          - ST. LOUIS, MO

" Look under your Boot, "Andy!" "

        DeAndre
          - St. Louis, MO

" 'You miss 100% of the shots you don't take'
                    - Wayne Gretzky "
                      - Michael

14

Cards Won! Opening Day! My Mrs.
is at home. But I'm in love with Kyle's
Sister. WTF. I'm Smitten. Fuck.

Love yourself before you love
anyone —

I Love and believe in
↑ (((

—

Start believing in one

ANOTHER

4/11/16

BOOMER is the best!! He took us to Taco Bell, which was amassing.

4/12/16

Boomer is wonderful!
I really enjoy him.
→ Thank you,

Lindsay from South City

John from Miami, FL
- Miami is being inundated
by Mexican Drug Gangs &
ruining the city!

Jason: I'm ~~too~~ busy to
From St. Louis / share my opinions or
thoughts. Gotta keep
making phone calls
in route.

16

4/9/16

So many lives are changed
by choice of virtue. life
is a choice, give it a chance
Many choose wrong. Robert
Frost chose right, One
place, one time.

4/10/16

Do what makes you happy.
You can't please everyone, so
why try?? Make yourself
happy. If you happen to make
other people happy on the
way, thats just bonus points.
                        Joe
                   (fenton)

4/1x | Amy. from Shanghai (wash univ student)

If you ever become fear of sth, you are merely fear of the fearness itself. So don't let fearness beat you up.

⌒

I am not raised in a Christian household so the weight of sins is an unfamiliar ~~for~~ burden. I think the things I fear are fears that have been ~~not~~ personally constructed.

I tend to think that sin should not be feared because it is — by defin — a human eventuality. We make mistakes. <u>Big ones</u>. It's not a how we screw up, but how we react to it that makes a difference. ~~If you~~ ~~~~ Sin, in the right context, is virtue.

—Aakash. WashU '16

Appreciating life is often a question of managing ones expectations of what life should be.

— Jason (San Francisco) 4/12/16

P.S. I'm with stupid

RUDE!!!

Live simply. All that you need is in your soul... and a bar of chocolate :)

Kim (San Francisco) 4/12/16

P.S. I'm with stupid-er!

Employee Friends

19

If your going to dream —
Dream Big!
Mary Billingsley — KC, KS
4/13/16 - When you're different, when
you're special, ~~sometimes~~ sometimes
you have to get used to being alone.
4/13/16 - Someone will always be prettier.
Someone will always be smarter
Someone will always be younger
But they will never be you
— Gwen 4/13 STL

"There's a day when you realize
that you're not just a survivor,
you're a warrior. You're tougher
than anything life throws your
way." ~ Brooke Davis One Tree Hill
Ella 4/13/16 St. Louis

"Really, I don't care if people think I'm too
skinny. This is my body. If they don't like
it, screw it." - Ellen Pompeo
— Emma 4/13 STL

20

1) A bit too much is just enough for me ~~[crossed out]~~

2) "You miss 100% of the shots you don't take"... Listen to the great One
   — Zander Wash √19' Westchester NY

3. "Too many people don't stop and think anymore. Put your phone down and talk to somebody you'll be better off for it in the long run"

4. Booze. Because no great story ever started with a salad.

"It pisses me off when the General public thinks the "rich" should pay higher taxes, its Already 39% compared to 18-25%. Last I check X% of a lot is more than X% of a little!

The Education System needs to teach high school & college age people how to show tolerance of opposite points of view.

4/13/16

"Can you remember who you were,
before the world told you who you should
be?" *

Always be your most authentic self.
There are so many people who will
try and tell you who to be yet you
are living your life, not them!
— Paul from Chicago!

"
To even know that one life has
lived and breathed easier because of you
is to have succeeded "
— My Favorite Quote

The secret of change is always to focus
all your energy not on fighting the old but
building the new. Brian C. Griffin Rd.

22

4/14/16

Don't live life as a victim.
Overcome your obstacles
Devon - STL

At the end of one's life, you will never
hear them say "I worked too little", "I loved
too much", "I spent too much time with my family".
Nike - STL

BE COURTEOUS & KIND
     - K.M, DELAWARE

Make every day more meaningful than the last.
     - A.S. , Boston

23

When you ~~know~~ don't know where you are going
and you have to pick between two routes, pick
the harder one. Don't go easy on yourself.

Wash U student
From Beijing, China

Success is knowing you could lose
~~every~~thing and still be happy.

—JR, WUSTL
sophomore

Good people in power do good
things; bad people in power
just make money

Tom ~~From~~ Cleveland

One day, a young boy asked
an old man: "Sir, which is the
best day to pray?" The wise old
man replied: "My son, the best day
to pray is the day before you die."
The boy was astonished and replied:
"Sir, how can I know the day of my
death?" The old man answered: "NO
one knows the day of his death, that's
why we need to pray everyday."

24

You're hotter anyways

History is written by the victor

The first step is the hardest – MS

Stop worrying about what you
can't change ... it'll only
keep you up a night –
Arin Wash U Student

I love to watch videos
from a guy named Casey
Neistat online. He travels the
world and manages a tech
startup and makes a video
everyday about it. I went
to a rural boarding school
and watching these videos
made less isolated
and and frustrated by
the monotony
Henry Wash U student

25

All people are equal in everything but politics fucks everything up.

Failure will never overtake me if my determination is strong enough

What you do today can improve all your tomorrows.

"All you need in life is a good friend, good wine, & good books"

"El amor no es moral ni inmoral"

"Learn to be comfortable being uncomfortable"

26

~~Be yourself~~

— "Be yourself, everyone else is already taken" ~~anon~~

~~Smile~~

Don't take anything for granted

You only go around once, Enjoy life.

Love

Laugh

Live

4/25/16

My Father is a huge inspiration to me B/C he has had his own business for almost 30 years now. he always overcomes the crap thrown his way

Wyatt S. ?....r
Overland / St. Louis Mo

28

4/27   something that's inspirational
        to me is the feeling of being
        outdoors early in the morning
        when most people are asleep—
        it's so peaceful.

                —Deepti, Atlanta, GA

4/28.   I am inspired by the books I
        read. —Charley Birk, Landenberg, PA

        Spring inspire's me! So
        aptly named to reflect
        how the warming sun and
        budding new life reenergize's
        the spirit.
                        Cheryl PA

4/28/16

Stay Strong Let Go and
Let GOD....

            Akiah
            ST. Lauis, MO

4/29/16 To be present, and aware
don't lose your power
to fear, or anger.

                        Matt St. Louis
           Los Angeles

4/27/16

All my friends that graduated highschool with
me in 2009 have graduated and keep on telling
me that I was crazy if I think I would go
through with my dream of becoming a trauma
surgeon ... well here we are 2016 and I am
a year away from graduating Med school.
" The people that make fun of your dreams and
put you down, are only telling their own stories
and insecurities" Don't Be Afraid to Dream !
- Razan , Jordan

4.27.16 | I PURCHASED A SMALL
BUSINESS WITH NO EXPERIENCE AND
QUICKLY REALIZED THAT ANYTHING IS
POSSIBLE EVEN IF YOU'RE NOT
SURE HOW. YOU CAN JUST, LIKE, DO
THINGS AND LEARN ON THE FLY.
SEEMS OBVIOUS NOW, BUT IT WAS
REVELATORY AND CHANGED MY PERCEPTION
OF WHAT'S POSSIBLE AND ACCOMPLISHABLE
ALSO, BEING OPEN AND UNDERSTANDING
THAT EVERYONE HAS SOMETHING TO
TEACH.

31

4/25/16 — 4/26/16

You'll never love anyone wholly
until you ~~first~~ love yourself as #1.
Work on yourself, it's hard But
its worth every second! ♡♡
                        Josey
        SLU   Nursing Student

"Do what you can, with what you have,
where you are.
                Theodore Roosevelt

It's never what you think
        Joe - S___

Don't forget what you originally want to do
                        Evan - Cali

Our deepest fear is not that we are inadequate.
Our deepest fear is that we are powerful beyond measure.
        Joe, San Francisco (4/27)

The best thing in my life are my parents
& my new born son, The greatest source
of joy for me — makes me realize
about the true beauty & essence of life.
                WK, St Louis, 4/27/16

32

My biggest motivation in life is
my family!... I took the wrong road
in life for many years but for some
reason my family never gave up on me.
I am a recovering heroin addict, 4 years
clean now! I will do everything in my
power to keep me and my family proud
of me! This is what life is all about.

Now 4 years drug free!,   Sabrina, St. Louis MO!

Do something with your life. Don't
join the Army. Join the Air Force.
                    Adam, St. Louis

I come from china. The biggest
moment in my life is I play
soccer match and I got the
champion.

MY CHILDREN KEEP ME TRUCKING
ALONG. WHENEVER TIMES ARE TOUGH,
I REFLECT ON MY SON'S LAUGHTER
OR MY DAUGHTER'S SMILE AND
I MOTIVATE MYSELF TO CONTINUE
ON.
                    Chris from KG

My biggest Motivation is success. Not
defined by money or wealth, but by
love and family. My grandfather, Seele,
instilled these beliefs in me young. He
was wealthy but always reminded and
taught me what really matters.

                    BRIAN, CHICAGO via DETROIT

My biggest motivation is having A
sense of Adventure, Exploring new places, And
sharing it with the friends & family I
love.

                    Rich, CHICAGO VIA NJ.

I am motivated by my
friends & family
AND I am also motivated
by FOOD! Yummmmy
Stacey StLouis

Find what makes you happy,
what you are passionate about,
and what will make you grow.
Davi StLouis
Monterey

I'm moved forward & motivated by
① Jesus + the purpose + calling on my life.
Understanding my past doesn't define me
but can be used to make a difference
in the world. The future/calling etc pulls
me forward as I keep my eyes today
ahead.

I am definately motivated by my
faith. God has called me to ministry,
and the change I see in my life and
others inspires me
Nathaniel

35

4/22/16 What motivates me is my friends. They constantly make me a better person & make me want to succeed in life. Whenever I doubt myself they pick me back up.

Emily   StLou

4/22/16 I'm motivated by my faith in Jesus.

Kelsi, StLouis

4/23/16 My life has been influenced by many experiences. When 4 yrs old I moved (on my b-day) to Lynchburg VA from StL. I was bullied by my classmates and the neighborhood kids because I was a "YANKEE". I returned to STL (on my 13th B-Day) and was glad to be back in STL, but unfortunately I had picked up a Southern accent in VA and the kids teased me and called me names like "Country Hick" etc. This motivates me to be kind to those that are different from me. I was diagnosed with Manic Depression (now called Bi Polar Disorder) at 11 yrs old at Duke University several hrs. from VA and had to stay there for what seemed an eternity... I was so so homesick!

Continued
⬇

(continued from prior page)

Then, I met a GREAT doctor by the name of Dr._____. He was so kind, patient, and understanding. He prescribed Lithium to help smooth out my ↑'s & ↓'s. He motivated me to live a fulfilling life. As of today I now have been married for an amazing 33 years! I now have two fantastic children with my very loving lovely supportive wife who still stands by me.

(Anonymous-St Louis)

IF you ALWAYS GIVE 110%
GOOD THINGS WILL HAPPEN
FREEDOM TO DO WHAT I WANT
TO DO, SUPPORT PEOPLE AROUND ME, ☺
GIVE BACK TO COMMUNITY
    - ANDREW   STL

My motivation is myself. I want to be someone and the only way I am going to make that happen is to keep being strong and willing. SCHOOL AND WORK is important to get me to this spot. MONEY is a motivation, also. Makes me WORK harder to get where I need to be!   tara *STL (A 3 TIME DWI offender)

4/22

(b'shem Hashem - with Name of G-d) ד״ז

22 April 2011

Life is a challenge - an opportunity to keep your brain alive, to seek solutions and achieve - whether its peace, prosperity, a goal, survival. The key is to have faith that a) we are but a speck in the universal picture and b) strong faith + good friends will elevate our hope.

Rabbi Shulamit
Atlanta, Chicago, Jerusalem

In my darkest winter ~~the~~ I've found in myself an invincible summer

Rob, St. Louis
South City

by Albert Camus

4/25

Life's tough, and it's always been. And I never regret to take this tough way. What motivates me basically are relationships and my "dream". I appreciate what my friends and family have given me. They'd been so supportive. They are the motivation when I'm ~~down~~ down. "Dream" is what I've always wanted to do. I don't even know if I can accomplish it, but I still make effort towards it. I do just because I like it. And I like it because I did it.

Senior
Student
at Wash U   Art/Architecture/Business   ℬ John from Beijing. China.

38

4/21

Bianca (Decatur GA, via STL)

Just turning 25 I've had my good share of hard times. From foster care to being homeless, I'm now a mother and stronger than ever. ? I want people to know matter how hard life gets, you can get through it. My daughter is my hero she motivates me so much I don't know where I'd be without her. Life will come at you fast you just gotta grab it by the horns and go. As my three year old says "Be glad you're here"

4/21

IF YOU WANT LOVE, GIVE A LITTLE
IF YOU WANT FAITH, BELIEVE A LITTLE
IF YOU WANT PEACE, TURN YOUR CHEEK A LITTLE

COTTON (ST. LOUIS, MO)

My mom is thee strongest, lovable,
selflesss person in the world. She
is my rock. She pratically raised
my sister & I on her own. while
working a full time job & going to
school. SOMEHOW made it to all
my basketball games & any other
activities I participated in. On September
all of our lives changed when
her husband, my step.dad, got into
a horrible farming accident. ~~the~~
~~debate serious~~. He was an
amazing man, father & husband.
I don't know whats harder -
~~the~~ the lost of a love one or
seeing someone you love so
much in horrible pain & not
being able to do anything to
ease the pain. My mom deals
with this pain everyday of missing
her husband. I want to give
her the world. Do anything
to ease the pain. And be
the best daughter, employee,
friend I can possibley be.

4/19/16

The number one person that has motivated me throughout the years has been my father. He has inspired me to strive for success in all aspects of life, especially through sports growing up and into a collegiate football career. I model my old man to always stay humble and to put hard work in, in order to succeed.

      — Thomas , Grand Rapids MI

4/14/16
Always trying to better myself & being a Man for others, Try to have fun each day.
      — unknown rider

4/9

Be kind to people.
Be kind to yourself. It's okay to
live a life others don't understand
Be happy. Spread happiness

Char, Chicago   Consultant

The Phrase, "do not be afraid" is
written in the Bible 365 times. That's
a daily reminder from God to live
every day being fearless.
          Lydia, Ladue

Why do we close our eyes when
we pray, cry, kiss, dream? Because
the most beautiful things in life
are not seen but felt by the heart.
          Lydia, Ladue
          Fitness Instructor

42

Jacob, Chicago — Let's play two!

Evan, New Jersey
"When you see a fork in the road,
take it."

4/9/16

Put one foot in frount of the other.
And take one day at a Time.
Life is not as bad as you think it is.
It's Just hard. ~~Skeet~~ / South City
St. Louis

Martin - ~~Argentina~~   Martín from
                                Argentina

Carpe diem. Be humble. Help others.
Inspirational ride.

BEING THE BEST "YOU" AS POSSIBLE.
                        Zad STL

Call Center Jobs
would be handled
excellently in US
            Saint Louis MO
Diane S
Love Uber

when you feel like quitting, think
about why you started. Tera St. Louis, mo

3D mammograms are the new technology i every
woman should invest in this. Breast Cancer is
being found faster! earlier! Tera St Louis.

5/17

My motivation is my family
and friends. My two dogs, too.
But mostly getting drunk with
my friends.

Paige, Carlyle; RL

4/18/16

This rider has realized the ~~more~~ more
sad and depressed I become the more
kind-hearted and giving I become in turn.
I find it very strange

Dylan
St. Louis MO

A job application once asked who my childhood ~~hero~~ was. I realized I never had one. So,
in response, I wrote:
"Anyone who can afford compassion for lesser
fortunate humans while not being taken advantage of"

JASON
ST. LOUIS, MO
SELF·TAUGHT

Rob, New York, NY

Life is full of ups and downs,
but I have realized that if you
stay true to yourself and always
work hard, you will get through
the lows.

Allie, Phoenix, AZ   SLU student; pre-med Double major in Forensic
① "Hello, Babies. Welcome to Earth. Its hot in ~~science &~~ science &
    the summer & cold in the winter. It's round psychology
    and wet and crowded. On the outside, babies,
    you've got a hundred years here. There's only
    one rule that I know of, babies - God damn it,
    you've got to be kind.'"
            - Kurt

The world is an imperfect place
But we need to keep striving for perfection
Or we will all will perish,
            From New York

4/18/16

Change is constant. Don't get too comfortable, but embrace the change + challenges that come with it.   -Clint, St. Louis, Mo

- Be the change you wish to see in the world
- A big shot is just a little shot that keeps shooting
                                        -Dee - NJ

DAVE FROM LOUISVILLE, KY
I wish I could have stayed longer. I could have "seen" a Cards/Cubs game.
     -Dave is blind & travels around the country selling equipment to schools that assist the blind & those with limited vision.

4/18/16

Power Mongering is the reason entitlements are unending instead of temporary assistance to those that need a hand up in life.

— A concerned citizen

Even Lions (the King of the jungle) can ~~be~~ succomb to Tyranny if you feed them fresh meat daily and gradually degrade the quality of the meat until they die.

— Anonymous

Those that give up Liberty for Security deserve neither.

— Benjamin Franklin

4/18/16

Always look @ the situation as if you were
going into battle. You wouldn't go to
battle without your team or ammunition —
Be Ready!   —Adam Farmington Il High school

Courge is not the absense of fear; rather the
understanding that something else is more
important   —Anonamys

The son is not guilty for the
sins of the father but rather responsible
for not repeating those sins
                    Harry Soon LittleRock Ark
                    & Farm owner in Tennesee

Teach a man how to
fish and he will never go
hungry ... Give a man a
fish and he will surely starve.
                    —Jesus?

Give a man a fish and you have fed
him for a day; Teach him how to
fish and you feed him for a Lifetime.

50

"Don't forget to fall in love with yourself first" - Carrie
       - Sara, Florida

   The worst feeling in the world, is regret. Tell that person how you feel, Take that shot. Just give 110% in everything you do so you never wonder "What if?" - Daniel

   I see now that the circumstances of ones birth are irrelevant. It is what you do with the gift of life that determines who you are - Mewtwo, Pokemon

   "It's a dangerous business, Frodo, going out your door. You step onto the road, and if you don't keep your feet, there's no knowing where you might be swept off to." - Gandalf the Grey

51

Everything will be okay in the end. If it isn't okay, then it isn't yet the end. ♡

Pete the Cat
"If you judge a fish by its
ability to climb a tree,
it will spend its whole life
feeling stupid."
@Melissa   -Dlathe, KS

Every cloud has a silver lining.
            Darcey - Kansas City, KS

Advice from a male friend
about me, as a single woman &plus size,
dating & underwear —...
    "Nobody expects to get you home,
unzip your pants & a size to pop
out so wear a thong, be
proud of what you've got!"
    no Granny Panties

    let's all be friend with each other &
    keep this world safe + peaceful.
            From Chicago   Ade. MD

53

4/15/16

It's something unpredictable, but in the end, it's right. I hope you've had the time of your life.   Alice - St. Louis

"THE FIRST PRINCIPLE IS THAT YOU MUST NOT FOOL YOURSELF AND YOU ARE THE EASIEST PERSON TO FOOL."
ROB, ST. LOUIS   by - RICHARD FEYNMAN

Everything and everyone has a time, a season, and a reason. Don't rush anything, it will come when it is time to come to you.   Linda in South City, St Louis

I have grown up to realize, if I stay focused and keep life Positive, and it all does work out!
                              Dorothy   St. Louis

People in your life can be temperorary You how ever you are in it until its over.
                    memphis TN - Victor Taylor

4-19-16
Tomorrow is another day to fix what happened today. The only conscious you have to live with is your own. What goes around comes around.   Cathi - Pella, IA

54

Girls are almost always appealing, for most of the time fun, but in my experience have never not been tricky. I may be drunk writing this but I thought I had girls figured out after my 21 years of life. I was wrong undoubtedly and the reason, is that girls are beautifully insane. Not hard not fall in love with
— Nick South City King

4-9-16
You can't move forward if you keep reliving the Past.
Shelly- Affton, mo

4-11-16
"I've learned that people will ~~forget~~ forget what you said, people will forget what you did, but people will never forget how you made them feel."
— Maya Angelou
Patrick, Albuquerque, NM

"Be kind whenever possible. It
is always possible."
- Dalai Lama
Nick, San Diego

This quote always keeps me going during tough
times. For me, it serves as a reminder that
every setback is an opportunity for a comeback
and that we go through the "lows" to be
ready and appreciative of the "highs". So,
here it is ...
"An arrow can only be shot by pulling it
backwards. So when life is dragging you
back with difficulties, it means that it's
going to launch you into something great.
So just focus, and keep aiming."
- Unknown
Anina, Kenosha, WI

56

John Frey   Chicago, IL
The Bible

The Bible, The Big Book, and
Bicipiling! :) P.O. , STL

4/29/16   I don't beleive in religion, so I guess
my inspiration is death. I'm motivate
by death because once we die, + there's
static and nothing, so that makes
every moment of being alive so
urgently important.
                    Isabelle, St Louis
                    "Psychology Major"

4/28/16

God will get you further then you think
                    Paul , St. Louis

57

4/27/16 My biggest source of inspiration, and more motivation/sense of integrity, is something my dad told me when I was young: Do what you say, say what you do. I have found that with that as a guide, I am straightforward, respected, & a good listener.

— Mike   Tucson AZ

Jardin just purchased by Rubbermaid / ?

My Boston Terrier "Bauer" (from the TV show "24" Jack Bauer) is my source of inspiration. He is back in Columbus Ohio dealing with an infection on his right rear leg. The Vet says he may lose the leg to amputation. Please let him be OK!

Josh from
Columbus OH

It may be raining... but there's a rainbow above you.
— The Eagles "Desperado"

Tracy!
& Louis

In regards to Uber

"I guess Saint Louis does care about limiting the amount of drunk driving. It only took ... forever." -Chris

"My mother, Mary "passed" (died) 4 days ago. She bought these Cardinals tickets for my younger brother, weeks ago. Mary would have wanted us to go. She knew we loved the Cardinals. Now we get to spend an afternoon together, as brothers. I'll miss you, Mom; you keep giving even after you are gone. Love you" -Steve

"Hey Pa, there's a roach" said Jessbe. "Yeah" said Pa. "You ever eaten roach?" "Nope, but I done eat

Wanted to write something kickass but I didn't.
ML - WG

~~Ain't got no face!~~

There are steel ships & wood ships
but the best ships are friendships
Joe - STL

We are what we say we are, excellence,
therefore, it is not an act but a habit
~ Matt - STL - Lindbergh HS

No man is an island
Sharon STL/KC

No veni vocari justo sed pecatores
in panite cium
Sam STL

Awareness is key. Be mindful of
yourself, others, and honor differences.
Live your life with quiet confidence.
— Liam — Minnesota

Know your limits and once in awhile
push past them.
Rex — Buffalo, NY

When life gives you lemons, paint that
shit GOLD
Maggie — Seattle

So we beat on, boats against the current,
borne back ceaseless into the past
— Rob, NY
— Gatsby

"YOLO — You Only Live Once" — Madison

4/29/16

Maia — Nashville, TN
I get my inspiration from the rain. When
I'm in my room with a mug of tea and
I look outside — everything goes quiet. And
I'm at peace. I can think of everything I
want to be and who I admire and I
am inspired to change, to evolve... to be
the best me.

4/29/16
Cecilia— Shezhen, China / Cincinnati, Ohio.
  I got inspiration from my past experiences and
      the stories I heard. I love stories and
      I love traveling.
      My favorite quote is "I believe in the
      Sun, even when it rains"
  Thanks for a good ride. !!

Happiness is a choice! Rhonda, Oregon
Work hard so you can play harder. Shane
& Rhonda,
Oregon

Don't sweat the small stuff, and most
stuff aint large. Erik, Chicago, Hawks 1-1

"Here comes the sun."
APRIL 28th, 2016
St. Louis, MO
Emily

7/28 My 5th grade teacher Mr. Webster.
He taught me how to lead and got
me interested in finance.
  - Justin, ~~꠸꠸꠸~~
  Chapel Hill, NC

4/28 "Bloom where you are planted."
  - Ellie
  Champaign, IL

4/28 ~ My mom who recently passed away
from cancer, she was very strong & I
think about her everyday.
  - Conciie, St. Louis MO

4/29 - Be Happy. Not because everything
is Good But Because you can
See the Good in Everything.
  - Sherry, Carlsbad, Ca

"If it is to be, it is up to me."

—Abraham Elkin, my grandfather

Josh ‾‾‾‾   Ft. Lauderdale, FL

"Find out who you are, and be
the best damn one you can be."

"You Are Enough".

—Brené   ~J.P. New York,
                                              NY

65

05/02/16

My father beat addiction and poverty to raise
a family and send both kids to college.
Adam STL

May 2nd, 2016

Keep good friends & family
close to you ~ Jodi L, Michigan

May 2, 2016
Most inspirational thing in my life is my
39 year old brother who is fighting Glioblastoma brain
tumor. He has an amazing wife & 4 awesome kids.
Unfortunately there is nothing more the doctors can do
and it's in God's hands now. He has fought hard
for 16 months & it's time for him to rest.
I hope I can be half the person he is
An amazing person who lives life to the
fullest. Stephanie D - St. Louis, MO

May 2
"Dont Be Disapointed When DJ ing
& Someone Says "Would You Play Smothing Good"
Because Thier Paying Your Salary"

66

Loving isn't the hard part... the hard part is accepting someone's love for you. Embrace it, never take it for granted.

— Kendall, Chicago/Milwaukee

5/7/16 # CHOOSE HAPPINESS

Ali
Milwaukee

No matter what "when life gives you lemons make lemonaid!

— Chelsea   Bloomington IL

TAKE A STEP BACK. BREATHE. I PROMISE, EVERYTHING WILL WORK OUT. EVERYTHING WILL BE OKAY.

Shelbey, STL

If it's to be, it's up to me. You make your own luck and fortune.   Jake, LA, CA

Let go! Let flow!   Stephanie Modesto, CA

4/29 "I've learned that its never too late to be what you could've been" - Roger

(microbiologist) ~~with~~ NJ now in STL

4/29 Don't forget to smile smile, smile.
- Grateful Dead
(Courtney ....) New York
& Amanda from San Fran

4/29 0 Even through the darkest times always look for the light at the end of the tunnel. Even when you think it's rough, just remember that some is going through something elle.
-Lauren, Fort Lauderdale, FL now st.Louis

5/1/16

My Brother Has his
Pilots License... hes only 16
what are you doing??
I PLay Make uP At AVEDA - Maya
SNAPCHAT
Insta
Twitter

5/2/16

My father had stomach cancer, but
he always had a smile on his face and
always cracked a joke whenever he could.
It Keeps me going when i think about
his passing. love the world & the People in it.
Tiara, from St. Louis :)

5/2/16
My brother, who is younger than I am,
has always been there for me. He has been struggling
with type-1 diabetes for most of his life, but
in the face of this adversity he has managed
to excel in career, sports and have a beautiful
family. He makes me want to get up and
go when I don't feel like it.
JAMES FROM St Louis

69

5/03/16

Hard work of the common people inspires me. Through actions like leaving your job and hiking the Appalachain Trail like my friend Jacob or putting in 40+ hours as a single mother. I invest my emotions in all and can be inspired by their day to day routines. Get out of your comfort zone!

Vittorio ~,...
Bartender/Server at
Italian Ristorande
Brentwood, MO

Don't quit. Its that simple, and that hard at the same time
Josh, St Louis

Your outlook on life is a direct reflection of how much you like yourself. So choose a positive thought.

www.lululemon.com   Katie, Seattle

70

From Detroit

Mary- No matter how dark it seems, keep moving.
The sun always comes out. Here riding today
on my quest to visit all 50 states before
I'm 50. Just turned 46 yesterday, 6 more
to go. The world has so much to teach
when you keep your heart + mind open to
everyone + everything around you. Someone
will always tell you it can't be done.
It's not true! Sometimes it just takes more
time. Keep walking + listen to your inside —
the only voice that matters.

Lisa — Allow yourself to be vulnerable.
take a chance & be open to new experiences —
open your heart and allow yourself to get hurt.
Always know you're going to be okay.
 From New York

Marla — Never give up . . . everything happens
for a reason. You are where you
are supposed to be. (utah)

Greed = The flood . . . Now this is the law of the

71

5/6/16 Always fight for what you believe in. Always. It makes the world cool.

I'm inspired by what's going to help people. I've always enjoyed standing up for those who get picked on for no reason. I want to save the world. That ambition inspires me to make the world a better place. Whatever that means.

- Kylan S.
Webster Univ. / Sociology Major

KS & KC Always

5/7/16
SATURDAY

I've been a teacher for the past 9 years and my student have been my biggest inspiration.

My Highschool - Quincy Notre Dame - Megan
College - Indiana University Webster Groves, Mo
"Go Hoosiers!"

72

5/7/16

"if you think you can or you think you can't, you're right"

We ARE iN this UBER oN ouR 5th annual Birthday trip for our friend & brother Matt T. from Spfld. I've never met anyone on their death bed that wished they spent more time at work, with that being said we take as many opportunities to get together and spend quality time with each other. Go Cards!   Ryan C
                                                      Scott S
                                                       Tanner S
                                                        Matt T

Shoot Rock - NE AR - color: 1920's
I didn't have to gas ↑ &
stock the fire as much!

Don't get Chlamydia or use
Glitter... they're both
a nuisance & hard to get rid of.

73

5/9/16

~~Rue~~ Drive from (L.O.V.E.)
Live. Once. Value. Everything (L.O.V.E)
— Tyrell T. , ST. LOUIS

Live in your Integrity - Love all!
— Kathryn , St Louis

Everything is fun, just make it that way
— Jared Lexington KY

If you aren't having fun, you aren't
living life
— Stacey, Iowa City

If theres a fork in the road, ask
Yogi Berra which way to go
— Dave, Iowa City

5/9/16

Work hard, love much, and take time to
enjoy family! — Ethan

5/11 People Whom inspire me:
        Kurt Donald Cobain
        Jimi Hendrix
        Michael Eugene Archer
        Christopher Breaux

74

5/9/16

Set realistic goals because
expectations are premeditated
resentments.
                                    Stefanie, STL

5/9/2016 I'm on a spiritual path, yoga is
my vehicle. I'm currently in a yoga
teacher training program, the most heart-
centered, spiritual & comprehensive tools for
life and for managing difficulties and
your emotions. I hope to share this
amazing healing modality with as
many people as possible. Meghan—Cuba,
                                        Missouri

5/9/2016
"Whoever you are, no matter how lonely,
the world offers itself to your imagination,
calls to you like the wild geese, harsh and exciting
over and over announcing your place
in the family of things."
                                    -from "Wild Geese"
(one of my favorite   )   by Mary Oliver
 poems (: -Mia _____)

75

Rohi
Illinois

Something I struggled with for a long time was being a victim of sexual assault. It occurred the summer before my freshman year by a very close friend of mine. I don't remember much, but I woke up next to her after a night of drinking while she was completely sober. I was depressed and confused for a long time. At the time, I thought a male could not be sexually assaulted and I was ashamed of what had happened because it seemed like my fault. I was too scared to reach out to anyone as I would put societal expectations of my masculinity into question. When the school year started, I passed by her on campus and she said "Are you ready for round 2?!" This hurt so bad. The fact that she hadn't realized what she did. I tried to commit suicide the week after, but my friends convinced me out of it. Fast forward a year, I am the happiest I have ever been with a girlfriend and my academics going well. What changed?

5/10/16

Felicia   From New York, USA

I was born with a hearing loss and
so right from the start I was put at
a disadvantage from my peers. Honestly,
I hated to be different from other people
and I would get annoyed when people pointed
at my hearing aids, constantly trying to hide
the existence of this disability. However, as I grew
older, I began to realize that our differences
make us who we are, and they don't hinder our
abilities. I was able to get into a great school
because of my hard work, and didn't let
my hearing loss stop me. Some advice to anyone
reading this: you can do whatever you set your
mind to as long as you work hard enough for it.
Hard work beats talent when talent doesn't
work hard.

5/10/16

You can survive so much more than you think you can. Everyone is fighting their own battles, so never minimize what it is that you are going through. As cliché as it is, I'll say it anyways: always reach out. This year I got out of an abusive relationship, and I felt so alone and ashamed and confused, until by chance I discovered that a girl across the hall from me had been through a similar situation with an abusive ex who also had antisocial personality disorder. Talking to her got me through this year. So my advice is to just always reach out, because there ~~is~~ is always going to be someone there.

~~████████~~

xoxo,

Ansley

5/10/16

The secret of change is to focus All of your energy not on fighting the old, but on building the new.

Kim

SOCKAtes   BocA RatonFl

78

Karena, MA
My motivation is my parents. They worked so hard to immigrate to the US and give me everything they could. I don't want that to go to waste! ☺

Katie, MN
My friends are my motivation. Individually, they all have a quality that I desire to have as well. I see them, and I see things that I can better in myself. ☺

Sanjit, IL

There are no bad situations, only poor attitudes. It's easy to just accept a situation as final & be unmotivated to change it or take advantage. Always be critical of yourself because that's the only person you have complete control over.

My sisters inspire me. I am the middle of 3 girls, and I love it. They are both so different and so radiant. Carly, the younger one, is positively brilliant - so smart, and hilarious if you listen close enough to hear her jokes. Lesley, the older, is spunky, loud & outrageousely confident. I aspire to be more like them each & every day. They are my best friends.

Haley (Cleveland, OH)

Chio inspires and motivates me a lot. She's my 17-year-old sister. She has Down Syndrom but she doesn't know the concept of "limit"; or maybe she knows it but she doesn't care. She is always practicing, fighting, and doing EVERYTHING she can to achieve her goals. I love how sassy, confident and strong she is; how much effort she puts on achieving her objectives and, most important, how pure, loving and amazing her motivations are. She is certainly an extraordinary human being.

Michelle (Mexico City, Mexico

5/12/16

Never give up. Seek out your
goals, even if it takes you until
your last day on Earth. Do
good.

Elizabeth Town Kansas City, MO

5/12/16

Theres only a few things you can control
in this life, most of it is thrown at you
and it's how you react that make you or who
you are. The 2 things you can control are
effort and attitude.

Also, always leave things in better shape
than you got them.

Craig Y St Louis

81

Casey
5/22
Freeman yr at college ... a time to
learn + grow. But one day my mom called
me telling me my grandma had passed. In that
moment I felt so guilty for not visiting Korea
that yr or even calling — despite my bad accent.
Family comes first and your words mean everything
when you can't see them.

⤷ also try Q wings plus
        — dope korean wings
⤷ Seoul Q + Garden = trash

    Seoul taco = mediocre trash

5/21 AJ - Washington, DC

I like the way I see the world when I'm in an unfamiliar place. Little, mundane things became more interesting. I want to try (and you should, too) to see my everyday life in this way.

5/21 Washington, DC   Laura

Explore the unseen. Talk to the underrepresented. Leave your comfort zone. Know no boundaries.

5/21 St. Louis, MO

The fear that you feel is not real.

As a teacher for the last 13 years, I'm motivated by the growth of my students & those kids I've worked with over the years. Teachers are very motivating & inspiring in my opinion. I'm also motivated by having a positive outlook on life & knowing there's a purpose & plan for your life. Be happy, help others, be the best you can be. :)

Leslie
St. Peters MO

— When you look in the MIRROR every morning — YOU have to choose your kinda day INSPIRATION comes for each and everyone of "US" — choose JOY, LOVE, HAPPY!! :)

Amy / Ginny
St Charles Kirkwood

84

5/10/2016

Keep true to yourself. At the end of the day, your vision and ideas are reflections of what you are inside. Even if it's not popular, stay true to you. It's the greatest journey of all.

— Charles R. St. Louis, MO :) ;)

5-10-16

Life can be like a book — It's more exciting when you can turn the page and start a new chapter. That's why I never read a book twice — you can't look back — turn the page and seek out the next adventure!

Mike, Brentwood MO

4/19/16

During my toughest times I turn to my mom. She
has been able to help me through everything, whether
happy or sad and I don't know where I'd be
without her.   -Rachel Saint Louis, MO

During my hardest times I remember that
God is good all time no matter the circumstance.
He never leaves us nor forsakes us.
                    -Kelsy St.Louis

4/20/16

Something that has helped me over
time is knowing that ~~there is~~ is
always worse. No matter how bad
things get or are. Someone else,
somewhere else is always dealing
w/ worse & that gives me a reason
to not stress or worry.
                    -Chester
                    Chicago, IL

Chad, Utah – near Salt Lake

The Herd

Now this is the law of the prairie
    as old and as true as the sky
And the bison that keep it will prosper
and the bison that break it will die
    as the creeper that girdles the
        tree trunk.
This law is the final word.
For   the strength of the herd
        is the Bison.
And   the strength of the Bison
        is the herd.
        NDSU '13, '14

Through Life No Matter How Bad
things in Life gets, if you Look
hard enough and evaluate all the
Bad you will be able to Find ~~something~~
Something possative to make
you Life better

                Craig
            Layton Ut

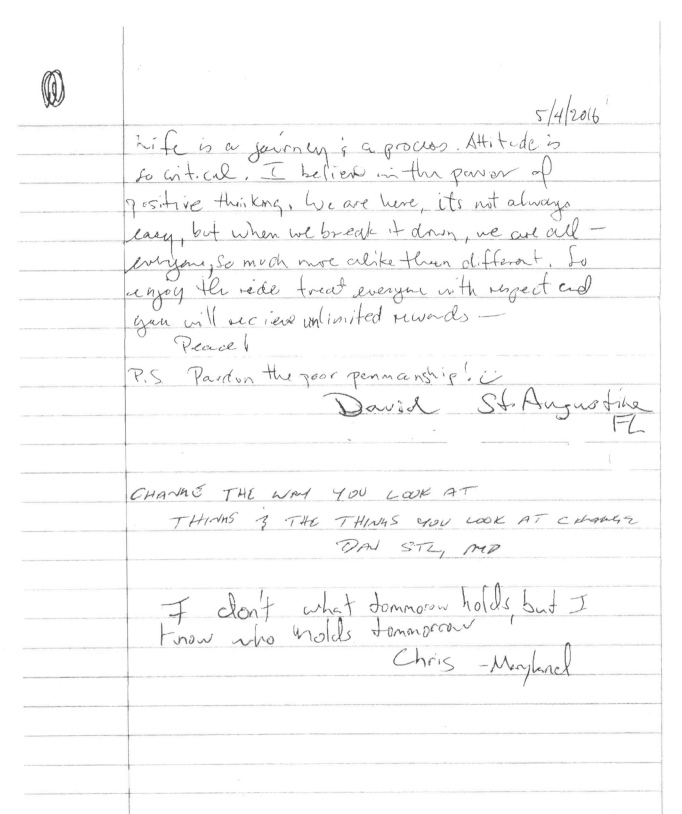

5/4/2016

Life is a journey & a process. Attitude is
so critical. I believe in the power of
positive thinking. We are here, its not always
easy, but when we break it down, we are all —
everyone, so much more alike than different. So
enjoy the ride treat everyone with respect and
you will recieve unlimited rewards —
    Peace !
P.S. Pardon the poor penmanship! ☺
          David   St Augustine
                        FL

CHANGE THE WAY YOU LOOK AT
    THINGS & THE THINGS YOU LOOK AT CHANGE
              DAN STL, MD

I don't what tommorow holds, but I
know who holds tommorrow
          Chris — Maryland

88

5/7/16

Things that require zero talent:
1) being on time
2) work ethic
3) effort
4) body language
5) energy
6) attitude
7) passion
8) taking advice
9) doing extra
10) being prepared
11) showing you care

Mazzi & Ryan
STL, MO

★ Recommended "Spare No Rib"
(near Hodak's)

4/29   Xing (Kayla) — Beijing + ½ Korea

     My inspiration of my life is my changing self. Like I like traveling & meeting new ppl and learn new things in general and values. :)

(AKA Cindy)

Ji-hyun Hur — Korea

     My inspiration of my life is the time that I've spent preparing myself for my future and getting ready for achieving my goals.

Melinda ~~Im~~ — Milwaukee

     I get my inspiration from my parents. They both came from very different backgrounds and they made their lives what they wanted them to be. Also I get my inspiration from my younger sibling, they are always true to who they are even if they aren't accepted by many people they are non-binary. Finally my middle school english teacher Ms. Etten got me into a lot of who I am today.

90

Know if you're the sort of person who is energized or diminished by doing things for others. Be that person.

The biggest thing that I believe can impact a person's life is to serve others and actually care about the people in your life. This starts with family, then friends, and so on. First though, you need to care about and serve yourself so that you can find happiness and joy in life so you can then serve others to bring & share joy and happiness in their life. You will feel love for your fellow human beings, and most importantly you will feel love for yourself and be able to get though those tough times + make the most of the best of times.

Ryan C , SLC, UT 5/12/16

5/13/16   Agnes, From Hungary
(Unable to write)

5/18/16   From my time in the USMC during the invasion of Iraq. "Rejoice in your suffering, for suffering produces perseverance, perseverance produces character, and character produces hope, and hope does not disappoint for God (PAUL) has poured out His love into our hearts @ PHX, AZ

91

My buddy Bill passed away after battling cancer. Inspired me to live every day to the fullest. He lived everyday to the fullest and was always very positive, never complained during his fight with cancer

Kirk (KC)

My motivation: a quote from a Mary Oliver poem:
"Tell me, what is it you plan to do with your one wild and precious life?"

Keren (Minneapolis)

A Dr. Seuss Quote:
"You have brains in your head. You have feet in your shoes. You can steer yourself any direction you choose."
This quote motivates me when I feel like I am not smart enough to figure something out or when I have to make a tough decision.

Emma (Minneapolis, MN)

Animan - Singapore

What motivates me during my college years are the sort
of issues my parents endured when they went to
college - limited sets of clothes, unstable access to
electricity, and other similar issues. But despite that
they did not falter one bit — so I shouldn't either
when faced with much more superficial things.

Kevin - Singapore / Shanghai / Toronto
My family motivates me to put everything I
have into school and everyday life. Making them
smile and seeing them be proud of me is
what keeps me going.

5-11-16
Adam - St. Louis, MO
My wife and kids motivate me to be the best
person I can be. Are my parents for the great up bringing
they provided me and always treat people the
way I want to be treated.

Jenna   NY, NY

  My mom is my biggest source of
motivation. She grew up in a 1 bedroom
house with 3 other siblings and her
parents. Yet she worked hard to get
a scholarship to go to college and
eventually send me to college. Her
hardwork, determination, and kindness
surprise me every day. I have
accomplished all that I have because
of her.

I am highly motivated and driven by success
and reaching my highest potential. I will not stop
if I don't feel like I have done my best job.
Through this I have been able to tap into parts of
myself, both socially, personally, academically, athletically,
etc, that I never knew existed. If you don't push
yourself to your highest potential you will never
know what you are truly ~~express~~ capable of and
how amazing you can be.
                    ~Rachel Wash U sophomore
                    from Florida   5/10/16

94

I self reflected for a long time
and finally came to come to terms with
my identity. I think the point
of this is to recognize how dangerous
it can be to disassociate with your
identity.

미국에서 공부중인 한국인 부부 입니다. ☺

지금 야구보러 가는중 입니다~

요승한 & 강성열   화이팅!!

현영 & 현석

We're student couple, going to watch Cards game!
Hope we have a wonderful time to watch
our fellow Korean MLB leaguers!

　　　　　　　- Hyun Suk &
　　　　　　　　Hyun Young

every day, try to give yourself compassion.
　　　　　　　　　- A.J, St. Louis

"The subversive intellectual came under
false pretenses, with bad documents, out of
love. Her labor is as necessary as it is
unwelcome. The university needs what
she bears but cannot bear what she brings."
- Fred Moten and Stefano Harney, "The university
and ~~xxxxxxxxxx~~ The Undercommons:
Seven theses." (2004).
　　　　　　　　　- Jordan, St. Louis

96

5/9/16

.being successful and disciplined and
making my way in the world and
getting respect from people
-Zach, St. Louis

5-17-16

"You've got a brain in your
head, + you have shoes on
your feet. Its up to you
on which direction you choose."
-Dr Suess.
-Mera B. , SO IL

My inspiration comes from my family.
I am greatly motivated by making them proud
but not only that, I think its important to also
be happy. Above all else.

- Tuapeua
Windhoek, Namibia.

5/10/2016

God is who provides me the motivation to
live and serve others because He gave me
an unconditional love that I was so
undeserving of. So, I know - by His
strength - I can love with abandon and
serve eternally the souls of all that I
encounter. God is powerful and He
is love; so, Love is powerful.
                    — Solome ji   (Wash U student)
                    → born in Ethiopia, raised
                        in chicago

98

Choose Happiness

5/3/16 Just choose joy. No matter whats going on - find the joy... you'd be surprised what a difference it can make.

Teresa, St. Louis MO
Lets Go Blues!

5/3/16

~~DISCOVER WHAT HAPPENS TO DISASTERS. BY YOU~~

A NEGATIVE CAN BE USED TO INSPIRE.
ITS NOT WHAT HAPPENED, BUT HOW YOU
HANDLE IT THAT MATTERS.
CORRY   ST LOUIS MO.

5/3/16

How ~~one~~ one perceives a situation
in most important. If ~~a~~ one
perceives it as a negative
he/she will miss the opportunity
to use ~~his/her~~ his/her creativity ~~as~~ and to
channel ~~your~~ energy towards
constructing something positively
wonderful!   Leonardo
                                    Naples, Italy

05/03/2016

LEAD BY DOING, NOT BY TELLING OR
YELLING — THE BEST WAY TO INSPIRE
OTHERS IS TO BE THERE, BE PREPARED
AND BE READY AND WILLING TO JUMP
INTO THE MIDDLE OF A SITUATION AND
MAKE THINGS HAPPEN FOR THE BETTER
                    — RICHARD — ATLANTA

4/29   I'm inspired by my past mistakes.
          — Matt   St. Louis, MO

Kseniia   I am Inspired by the book
Russia   „The secret"

                  (Husband is Hockey Center
                    with Chicago Wolves
                    Blues Farm club)

4/29   "Eat, pray, love."
           Carolin & Baby Emma
           from Germany via Boston

4/29   Luck is when opportunity meets
    preparation.
              — Daniel
              St. Louis, MO

Mimi P. 4/20
Something that has helped me
over the year would be my
family member because they
have motivate me to go to school
and do better. And with the help
of God, I believe I can do anything
through christ himself.

Robin 4/20
I am most motivated by my parents. They
worked very hard with limited resources to make
anything possible for my brothers and me. When
I found education or work overwhelming I
think about their sacrafices.

Sara 4/20
When I was 12, my sister passed away
and was an organ donor. She saved
a woman's life across the country.
So organ donation provides hope to
individuals and communities, and has
helped me find motivation even in
the darkest times.

The biggest regret in life is wondering how things could've been if you would've taken that one chance.

Many times, doing the thing that sounds the scariest or most intimidating actually ends up being the most worthwhile.

Danielle, Denver

Self-Advocacy is the best form of self-love. You have to be the sun, in order to shine for others

Fabiola

Journey: Guatemala born, raised in NJ, college in Boston, Houston teacher, St. Louis grad school, NYC based.

"If there's a will there's a way."

May the talents be on your side!

Begin, I didn't cringe nd I piece y on a girl at harkes so it wast gll bd. See ya ar nne -Den Kom

103

Tim 4/20. (Melbourne, Australia)

My main motivations would be my faith in God, which is a fairly recent thing. I'm also motivated by my Dad. He died 13 yrs ago and he was a great man. He taught me the value of honesty, integrity and the need to work hard in life. I'm motivated to try and be like him.

Todd 4/21 (St. Louis)

As a pediatric oncologist, my biggest source of inspiration comes from the patients I treat. These kids get so sick but handle their illness with such grace and acceptance. Thankfully, the majority are cured and get back to being, happy, healthy, silly kids.

Marlene 4/21 (Washington, DC)
Be militant about your happiness.

5/5/16

JORDAN - ST.LOUIS VIA JOPLIN

THINGS HAPPEN FOR A REASON. SOUNDS CLICHE BUT
TOO MANY TIMES, IT HAS COME TRUE. LIFE IS TOO
COMPLICATED FOR ANSWER TO GET. LOVE YOUR FAMILY
+ FRIENDS + EVERYTHING ELSE WILL SORT ITSELF
OUT.

5/5/16
GRANT - ST. LOUIS
     MY FATHER IS MY INSPIRATION
THE MAN DOESN'T QUIT. HE IS AN
ENGINEER THAT WORK WITH FURNITURE
HE LIVES WITH DIABETES. I HAVE
ALWAYS BEEN AN ATHLETIC TYPE
AND NEVER HAD A PROBLEM WITH WEIGHT
THAT IS MY MOTIVATION TO STAY
IN SHAPE. TODAY I AM AN ENGINEER
WITH A NURSE PRACTICIONER FOR A WIFE
AND WE ARE ABOUT TO BUILD A HOUSE
LISTEN TO YOUR FATHER...
THE MAN KNOWS HIS SHIT!!!!

105

5/10/14

You can survive so much more than you think you can.
Everyone is fighting their own battles, so never minimize
what it is that you are going through. As cliché as it is,
I'll say it anyway: always reach out. This year I got
out of an abusive relationship, and I felt so alone and
ashamed and confused, until by chance I discovered
that a girl across the hall from me had been through
a similar situation with an abusive ex who also had
antisocial personality disorder. Talking to her got me
through this year. So my advice is to just always
reach out, because there ~~is~~ is always going to be
someone there.

~~xxxxxxxxxxxx~~
xoxo,
        Ansley

                                    5/10/16
The secret of change is to
focus All of your energy not on
fighting the old, but on building
the new.   Kim
        SOCKAtes   BocA Raton, FL

106

5/1/16

Jason - St. Louis
My biggest inspiration is Chelsea's
job. She works for family
services and she trys so hard
to keep families together it truly
inspires me!

Nora + Wolfgang from Stuttgart Germany
my Sister is an inspiration.
doing a great job for
refugees from Syria in
Germany, helping others
- my hard working father
was always an inspiration

Natasha - Springfield, Mo.
    I wish more people would try
to empathize before judging. Open your
heart + mind + amazing relationships
will happen. (Massage Therapist)

107

"Do what you love, find out what you're good at, and go make a living doing it" - Ben ~ ~~~~, Los Angeles & ~~St. Louis~~

"Education is the passport to the future for tomorrow belongs to those who prepare for it today"

Tia,
Chicago

AGE IS ONLY A MATTER OF MIND. IF YOU DON'T MIND IT DOESN'T MATTER

STEVE,
THE GROVE

5/17/16

2 Friends that met Volunteering

— Onaedo & Z   5/17/2016   S. AFRICA

Meetings by chance change lives.

Take the opportunities that come
your way! You dont know   :)
who you'll meet,
And you won't know how you'll
change.

5/19/16

In conversation w/ my heavenly
Father, He told me simply that
He is proud of me ... no need to
strive

Nona NONA
        Austin Tx, via mariette lam

05/16/2016

James,
London,
UK.

You have 1000 months of life. 1000 months awake. And there is no other life beyond this one; this is your one shot. There is no God, no Plan, no Secret; only you, your choices. Your life.
Live well. Live now. Or you will not live at all

Be kind. Be humble. Be well.
Love wrecklessly. Give to others. XO Laura Hodges
Life is all about people, choose wisely &
Show up!

5/16/16

Be your true self.
You're worth it!   XO- Alex R.
                                                    STL 5/16/16

Stephanie
STL MO

You are fearfully & wonderfully made

Colleen
Kansas
City.

You are where you're supposed to be.

111

June 1, 2014

It's not usual at times for a greyhound driver to inspire his ~~driver~~ riders to spread positivity and live a positive life. The best and the most inspiring ride of my life it has been, from Chicago to St. Louis. The gentleman simply concluded by saying "If you cannot 'change' the people around you, change the people around you" and there comes St. Louis. Every stop has inspired us equally thou Every announcement was followed by an easy moment. This has inspired me to spread positive at even the simple moments.

— Nithisha
India

112

It was not easy for me to digest the fact that even in todays generation there is no security for girls. I was shocked to hear that a girl was kidnapped by a group of men and she had to do something to save herself. The only thing she could do to survive at that point of time was acting to be possessed. She acted as if she was posed to come out of the situation. The thought process to save herself somehow has inspired me to get out of my very little problems compared to her.

- Mareesha
  Indian

113

Despite the news, the world is becoming a better
+ gentler place.

See Angels of our Nature
By Stephen Pinker
for inspiration 🙂

114

6/2/16

As an international student, I have met many difficulties, both culturally and in many other aspects. I am very lucky to be in a class which all of my classmates are friendly, and trying to make me feel envolved. (I am an graduate student at SLU in comm department, we have small class size so there are about 10 students in total). They would ask my opinion when we were discussing, find a topic for me when I seemed not envolved, and invite me to parties and so on. I love my classmates :)

Jinghan.
Kunming City, China
&
Saint Louis, U.S.

My grandfather always told me that it's more important who you're with than what you're doing or where you are. To me, that idea 100% rings true. The people you surround yourself with are one of the biggest drivers of your meaning and happiness in life.

Allie
Philadelphia PA

Just because people don't understand you, doesn't mean there is something wrong with you.

— Paul - St. Louis

115

Just be happy whatever situation your are in take all the people whome you love with you and respect you Mom and Dad always. This just a tip for a happy life.

Poranathi ☺

My grandfather who recently passed away always used the acronym "LVC." He said with Love, Values and Confidence, you can do anything in life.

Morgann. - STL

Becoming ~~and~~ parents of ~~our~~ kids who play chess ~~completely~~ and compete on world levels was an unexpected development that defined much of our lives. And we're happy about it!

G.B. (Western)
Guy (Ukraine &)
(seattle)

Whatever you can do or dream you can, begin it.
Boldness has genius, power, and magic in it.

- Goethe

- Morgan, San Diego

116

You will face Adversity. But Regardless of what disaster, tragedy, or loss has befallen you *Never* lose sight of how very many blessings you have. your health, your very life, Indeed, you are blessed to be alive this very day. It could end at any time. No matter how bad you think you have it, there are millions out there with so much worse pain, suffering, tragedy. You Are Blessed!

Cyril
Sugar Creek, MO 6-3-16

117

6/3/14

Don was right on time, personable a a safe Driver. We love Uber!. Not disappointed with the trip! Dicne a Halim
Valdosta, GA

Family and good people I work with motivate me. I love interacting with good people every day.
Donald, thanks for a great ride!
George F

I gain my inspiration from watching my son grow into a young man and find himself in this crazy world.
Gerry

My Inspiration lies in the visualization of improvement in both myself and my friends. Seeing others blossom alongside you is the most special experience. So make friends and accomplish goals with them and life becomes all the more amazing.
Dhiren
Naperville, IL

118

As a child of a first generation immigrants, I'm inspired by my parents who sacrificed and moved to a completely new universe, where, to this day aren't fully accepted. I strive to take advantage of every opportunity given what they had to do to get me them.

-Asif

First the colors, then the humans, that's usually how I see things or tend to.
Aei
Pakistan

My father gave me the gift of music as a child. Our bond as fellow music lovers has gotten us through times that could have torn other families apart. I moved away from home 6 years ago now working as a professional musician. Tonight he's seeing one of our favorite singers. I wish I was there too.

- NYC a BK 2016

119

Studying abroad when I was 20 (1980)
changed my whole perspective on
life and opened up a world
I had no idea existed. It made
me tolerant and open to new ways
of thinking. The world is really
a very small place and America
is not necessarily the center of it
Dan 6-3-16
Chicago, IL

6/8/16

— Shameeka/ St.Louis, MO 06-08-16
As a child I always knew that
I wanted to be a mother. So I had
my first child when I was 18 years old.
And as much as I wanted children,
to this day I only have one child.
Her dad is now in the U.S. Army
and really don't do anything for her.
I have tried to get help as far as that
but people tell me that since he is out
of state there is nothing that they can
do until he comes back. Which no one
knows. So I have been a single mother
for all of my daughters life. Its not so
bad, because any time I be down my daughter
is such a great sprit she makes everything better.

120

6/8/16

I have learned that no matter how dark or bad things are, that there is always bright light and things will get better. The key is faith and ~~that~~ a friend to lean on.

Jim
Fredericksburg, VA

June 10, 2016

I'm always trying to be happy and motivated. Hard times will alway be there, that is life. Its how you take these hard time ~~and use the only~~ use them as learning experiences. ~~Just to your~~ I always try to move forward and push to be a better human. I lost my mother in a traggic accident when I was 21. I'm 26 now and I have push myself so hard to make her happy! I'm so happy with my current career choices, the wife I have chosen, and where I am at today. My mother keeps me motivated every day. I will always be motivated because of everything she taught me. I want to be the best person I can be, all because of her!

Preston ... St. Louis, MO

"If you're going through Hell, keep going."

— Winston Churchill
(supposedly)?

— Keara
San Diego, CA
6/10/16

"For the wages of sin is death, but the free gift of God is eternal life in Christ Jesus our Lord."
— Romans 6:23, Holy Bible
Kial, Alabama

You are not the product of your circumstances. You are a composite of all the things you believe, and all the places you believe you can go. Your past does not define you. You can step out of history & create a new day for yourself. Even if the entire culture is saying, "You can't." Even if every single possible bad thing that can happen to you does, you can keep going forward.

O.W.
Hannal, Webster Groves

123

"THE GOAL IS TO REMAIN IN A
CONSTANT STATE OF DEPARTURE
WHILE ALWAYS ARRIVING"

— RICHARD LINKLATER
— ADAM BERKOWITZ

I WAS ADDICTED BUT NOW I AM
CLEAN ~~WITH~~ BY LOVE I ~~AM~~ AM
MARRIED + HAVE TWO KIDS!
GOD IS GREAT!
—Kevin

"In the 17th Chapter of Saint Luke it is
Written "The Kingdom of God is within man

Not one man, nor a group of men but in
All men, In you - the people."

The Great Dictator - Charles Chaplin

Lover Loveless

True growth happens outside your comfort zone.
Get comfortable being uncomfortable.

Jon _o..S

124

On a motorbike tour cross country, to raise money for Lifeline ministries childrens home in Haiti. Children are the future

King
Cincinnati, OH

The elders teach the younger generation.

At Cincinnatti, OH

Work in Haiti most of the time. Helping the kids down there is my motivator to put together the Hogs for Haiti Motorcycle rides www.lifeline.org/hogs

Joe N. Carolina

Adversity is my strength. When I was younger I was small and smart and relentlessly bullied. Now I find myself in a position of relative power and try to stop bullies when I can.

Fairview Hts, IL
Matt

125

6/13/16

The biggest motivation for my life has definitely been my family. As the son of a first generation Mexican-American mother and Mexican immigrant father, not much was ever expected from me, by the rest of the world. However my parents never agreed with that. They have always pushed me and encouraged me to be better than they ever could be. They have ~~so~~ struggled and sacrificed so much to give me and my brother a life full of opportunity that they never really had. As a result, I am a year and half away from recieving a dual degree in engineering.

-Daniel, Kansas City, MO

6-13-16

As the oldest son of parents who grew up on farms, I have a unique appreciation of hardwork and long term goals. My mom and dad are truly inspirations to many. They both grew up poor and decided they wanted a better hope for themselves. College was out of the question so they both found good jobs, worked hard and lived frugal. My parents never spent money recklessly but my brother and I never suffered. Both my brother and I were able to graduate college with no debt thanks to our parents. That freedom has allowed us to pursue our dreams. The American Dream is alive and well for those prepared to EARN IT!

Kevin - St. Louis MO

126

8/14/16

Falling down is a natural part of life. It's even introduced to us at a very young age. I have an 23 month old and an 8 month old. They have fallen over a million times. They will probably fail one hundred million more times. Yet every time they know instinctively to get up. As an adult we often forget that in life we must get back up. Whether there is something that knocks us down, we must get back. When we put ourselves in situations that set us back, get back up. It's really quite simple, GET BACK UP!!

Blake, St. Louis, MO

6/14/16

I think that we need to be more mindful of our ability to change the world by small deeds each day. Maybe that small gesture might make the world of difference to someone else. In America all is possible yes but we don't all start at the same point so we need to be cognizant of the need to help others. In doing so we all rise together. More time should be spent on understanding that we all have a responsibility for each other.

Anonymous

I am very shy.
I am tiring to overcome my shyness
How I am doing that is opening myself
more to strangers and starting conversations
Sometimes I like fear keep me from being
the wonderful person that I am.

ARRIL
Kansas City, MO

As a History teacher I always tell my
students what Kennedy told us about the
moon. We don't do it because it is
easy, but we do because it's hard

CN 6/14/16

129

To Women —

    Don't lose yourself trying to gain self worth
from your ability to attract men. Allow your mind to
explore → push yourself in that way. If someone
in your life is stopping you from doing that —
especially a romantic partner, move on. Your
experiences are worth the heartache.

Skylar,—

130

Creativity requires courage — live, love, follow your passions, as God leads.

Michael, Denver

One quote I live by daily is "When you want to succeed as bad as you want to breathe, then you will be successful". — (from Eric Thomas.)

Deerra, St. Louis
by way of Philippines

"Try to embrace the worst moments of your life because those moments will shape and define you for the rest of your time on earth"
— Brandt

Grand Haven, MI

"First step is admitting your problem. Second step is waiting until after college to do something about it"

Jess, St. Louis

It's only embarassing if you care what people think

Sandra, Chicago, IL

6/15/16

"What Would it Look Like If we Started
over, I as a chef I ask myself this Daily
in a World with a broken Food System,
we need to Start over, Cleaner, better, Tastier!!

—Zach T.....
Charleston, SC

"I've always upheld the standard of being
optimistic no matter what's the situation. I find
that people who lack optimism aren't able to
dream big and therefore don't lead fulfilling lives.
I hope everyone in the world takes a moment
to pause and reflect."

—Brian ....
Seoul, Korea.

The meaning of public service? That is a hard question
to answer - if a question at all. I look at our world
today, and think this can't be the nation we want to
live in. I also look at our participation level &
the people we choose represent our interest. We are
a collection of everything we hoped to accomplish in
this country, and everything we feared ≋ we'd
dissolve into. JFK once said: "Let every nation know,
whether it wishes us well or ill - that we shall pay

any price, bear any burden, meet any hardship, support any friend, oppose any foe, to assure the survival + the success of liberty. This much we pledge, and more." I still believe we are that county. I still we believe we are public those people. This is what I define as ~~public~~ service.

J.P. Johnson
St. Louis Native

For me, my past has been influential. I've had to grow up fast & lived w/o parents between 6-9th grade because mom got sick. After she passed my dad kept telling me to live life to to fullest

① 6/15/2016 — Angel from Detroit by
way of NC

"Never let your fears decide your fate"
a motto I live by. Through travel
and adventure I've kept this thought
close to me as to remember that if
I allow myself to be healed back by
fear, I could very well allow myself to
let go of what could be the best
experience or opportunity of my life. It
speaks not only to travel and adventure
but also to so many aspects of life —
love, career, faith, race, etc. It's served
as a way to be more open minded, and
available to what life throws at you
as a reminder that you can work
through anything. This concept first
shook me when I booked my first solo
trip to central America — while I
felt nervous and others said I was
crazy to go somewhere so dangerous —
It turned out to be the best experience
of my life and I truly believe I am
a better person for it.

to conclude = buy the ticket, take the
ride.

6/16/16

My dad always told us
growing up that nobody
owes you anything. Earn
your keep, work hard.
(Also Be nice to people)
Because thats the only thing
free in the world.

Lynn
Corpus Christo Texas

Been inspired by how when there is
so much change in life - if you use it
as an opportunity to grow and to create
then magical thing start to happen
and you find joy in the moment &
realize just how amazing life truly
is
                Andrew #STL via UK.

135

6/16/16

You are in charge in your life
one moment you let someone control,
you is the moment you lose
control of your life. don't be
afraid to stand. find what
matter most to you and achieve it.
Michelle — Missouri

6/8/16

WRITING IS HARD. THAT NEVER STOPS. BUT
YOU CAN DO IT. THAT'S HOW EVERYONE ELSE DID.
#FIGHTON
RODNEY FROM
CA.

6/8/16 My grandmother is inspiration. Raised my mother
as a big single mother in poverty. Went back to
school as an adult, I remember going to her MOR
graduation when I was 5 years old. I have dinner with
her every Wednesdays and she keeps me focused.

6/8/16 inspiration is providing for your future family
before they're even here.
Brit from
North
Carolina

6/8/16

6/9/16 My call was very quick
and very good and Last Hamcadal
Bosnia

6/9/16 Positivity will make you a better person
Suzanne
Fenton MO

137

Todo estbo exelente el conductor
muy amable

Y quiero hacerles saber que no
tomo taxi mas solo Uber

——— o —— o —— o

Ebrithig is exelent
the draber was exelent to

and i want to thel everiguan
I not taking taxi enimor I taKing
uber

Panama City

Jaiqueline

+ Be Yourself

Derek
St. Louis

138

I've always ~~been into~~ had issues with trust. Knowing that God has my back helps me thru so much. I've lost many people in my life only at the age of 18. My struggle and suffering has helped me to better accept God and his influence in my life. I listened to a podcast once and heard this and its stuck with me. Its all by Grace and its all through Faith. Marnise, St. Louis

6/17/16

THE SMALLEST ACT OF KINDNESS CAN MAKE
A DIFFERENCE IN SOMEONES DAY.

Clay & Haley
Mt. Vernon IL   Birmingham. AL

6/30/16

My story was not the easy one, I have faced many hurdles and challenges in my life. I have to manage the complete finance expenses. Of my family, I had to fight hard for my marriage, my own development in the organization; my travel for right opportunities. Life has taught me to fight hard for my growth, development. Come Back, Get Back is the point of success, when life test you it has Same greatness in store for you. So work hard for the life you wish, Fate will also bow before your determination and hard work.

Naresh.
India.

Being of service to others is the key to my happiness. Working w/foster kids to

140

It's just nice to be nice. You never know what a person is dealing with. Just a simple hello or smile can turn a person's day around

Jackson W___
Memphis, TN

It comes down to perspective. You can have the worst day and make it your own.

John, Philippines

Just... stop caring.

- Zach, St Louis.

141

Boise 6/20/16 St. Louis, MO; Nigerian parents

One of the most motivational things for me was preserving the Current River. A few years ago, this river was in danger of being a pollutant. A toxic wasteland. I once saw a guy changing his oil in the river. This infuriated me. I immediately wrote an exerpt for many newspaper articles expressing my disappointment/disbelief for what the gentleman was doing. I was not able to change much at the time other than making him stop, but later I realized that my actions started a movement. Later on, I was responsible for new provisions written to protect the river. Now the Current River is thriving w/ both natural life & visitors respecting the natural grounds. A very proud moment in my life.

June 21 -

If I were to share words of wisdom today (I say today because if you asked me tomorrow, it might be very different) I would say: Trust in yourself and trust others — the world — the vibes around you - your gut instincts - your own self worth — and if you're able to do that, so much of everything else falls into place.

Along with that I would say - although this goes without ~~saying~~ - be kind, be generous, to others & to yourself. ~~Nothing is gained by a lack of generosity.~~ It's a win-win way to live and make life better for yourself and everyone around you.

Do I follow my own advice? Not always — ~~but~~ I try.

Scarlett
(LA)

143

Sandeep (Bangalore - India)

The need of the hour in the chaotic world we live in is to achieve individual peace, through which universal peace becomes possible. The way I found peace within myself was by looking within, through the practice of meditation. This helped me look at the world outside in a more joyous & positive light.

Each moment is unique and every second is priceless. Savor each and every ~~any~~ moment because once it has passed the time cannot be reclaimed. Make it count!

— Daniel ████████ (New York City

Do what you can with what you have where
you are...
Where the fuck am I?
Lindsay W.
St. Louis MO - Tower grove pk.

Ships don't sink b/c of the water around
them. ships sink b/c of the water in them.
Don't let whats happening around you
get inside you + weigh you down.
Kristin
Bobbie
St. Louis

6/22/16

I am inspired by the life of Rep.
John Lewis of Georgia

— Elizabeth N.Y.

Life is full of twists & turns and
each comes unexpectedly. My husband
is a daily inspiration to me. Watching
him overcome new obstacles on
a daily basis. Together we draw
strength from each other & our
faith in God.

God Bless
Teresa

22 June 2016 Poplar Bluff, MO

1/23 (Todd - S.F.)

IN 3 WORDS I CAN SUM UP EVERY THING I'VE
LEARNED ABOUT LIFE : IT GOES ON...
                                    ROBERT FROST

~~COACH~~ DAD
HAVING MADE ~~MY~~ CHOICES, LIVED THROUGH
CONSEQUENCES + HAVE LOST LOVES, ~~PARENTS~~ PARENTS
+ THINGS, I REALIZED LIFE DOES GO ON
+ IT WORKS ITS SELF OUT. YOU REALLY CAN'T
TURN BACK THE ~~TIME~~
                    CLOCK.

1/23 (Sabrena SF)
making a difference everyday,
everytime in the lives
of others

147

1/23 (Todd - S.F.)

IN 3 WORDS I CAN SUM UP EVERY THING I'VE
LEARNED ABOUT LIFE : IT GOES ON...
ROBERT FROST

HAVING MADE ~~GOOD & BAD~~ CHOICES, LIVED THROUGH
CONSEQUENCES & HAVE LOST LOVES, ~~PARENTS~~ PARENTS
& THINGS, I REALIZED LIFE DOES GO ON
& IT WORKS ITS SELF OUT. YOU REALLY CAN'T
TURN BACK THE ~~CLOCK~~ CLOCK

0/23 (Sabrena SF)
making a difference everyday,
everytime in the lives
of others

6/24/16

Fight for your own voice. Understand your place in your community. We all have the power to influence and change. As a musician I share sound energy with the world, hoping that in the moments we cry together, laugh together, rage together — we find our deepest and most artistic humanity. In these moments these journeys and connections, short and long we along with God define the contour of our reality.

Dave Eggar

NYC

Keyboard & Cellist for Phillip Phillips tomorrow night at River City

149

6/27/2016

You can learn something from anyone.

Every little thing is gonna be alright

It's okay to hit rock bottom. Perspective is everything.

— Nick (StL)

Treat everyone with kindness, for you have no idea what demons they are fighting. & you just might make their day.

"maybe sometimes the best thing to do is stop trying to figure out where you are going and just enjoy where you are" - SCRUBS

— Katie b STL

You look @ someone dancing. What they're thinking, how they're acting, they're alive act pure & free. They think their clear glass is thick walls, but it knew if that'll be the only time you see them in your whole life.

— Nick StL ("Ev")

150

"Not all who wander are lost."

-Shannon S. 6/21

"The future is whatever you shape it to be."
-John P. 6/21

Never let someone define your self-worth.
No dream is too big. live your life.
-Jenna STL/CHI 6/24

"Let your heart sweet heart be your compass when
you're lost". Let your heart be the prettiest thing
about you and stay loyal to yourself.
-Lauren B. STL 6/24

The most important thing you can do
is be kind.
Dee S. STL 6-29

6/27/16

An English lady who came to Nigeria as our English teacher motivated me as a teenager. I learnt that hard work could lead one to the top. I still remember her name - Ms Gready. Indeed my classmates said I tried to walk like her! She was a fantastic lady.
I owe my achievement in life to God and to her.

Beatma from Nigeria

I believe that it is good to be nice and kind to people at all times. When you think you are being kind to people, you are in fact being kind to yourself. When you invest in people, you are investing in yourself. Always pray for God's guidance.
Fortunatus, Nigeria

152

June 27

My Daughter once said
"Her Loveliness is taller than her bones"
it is something i aspire to represent

Adam - Philadelphia Pa

June 27

"Winter is coming" John

June 27
Grieving isn't a lonely unless you're alone
You see So I must seek the comforts of home
I must seek the comforts of home for I'm told
That the home is where the heart still lives.

6/29/16

"There is a crack, a crack in everything. That's how the light gets in" Leonard Cohen

    Jennifer - Boston

"You're never going to know the outcome if you don't ask her out."

    Brian — Korea.

No matter where you come from and no matter where you're going, the right words to anyone can turn their day and life around.

    Hugh - Chicago

"Black care rarely sits behind the rider whose pace is fast enough."

    - Theodore Roosevelt.

    Jay - STL

Don't dwell on the past, it will never come back. Focus on the future & enjoy everything and everyone that comes your way.

    Margaret, Los Angeles

154

I went back to work in order to let me have more opportunities to travel with my grandchildren. My grandchildren make me feel so young again. I get to see them discover new things that make them happy. Nothing gives me more pleasure.

Jeff

Chesterfield Mo.

Coin James,

When My first and amazingly beautiful girlfriend Meg Knott broke up with me, I was devestated. She was the love of my life and she left me on the curb At first I was sad, downright depressed and contemplated suicide. I tied a rope to my ceiling fan and tried to hang myself, but the rope broke and I took it as a sign from God that I was meant to live and love again. I tried men for awhile but it didn't really work out because I didn't really like dudes, but it was pretty hot. I've been speedating but I've only met guys so far, because no girls speeddate. while I still can't find love, I know one day that I'll find someone who loves me some day.

John, STL

My Mom had a friends die in 9/11. It was hella sad. Destroy ISIS

Thomas C

My stupit uncall fill tried to make me a sandwitch and it truly motivates me because his sandy's aren't even good. know what i'm sayin?

Eamonn H

"You miss 100% of the shots you don't take"
- Wayne Gretzky
- Michael Scott
- Eamonn Horgan

Lindsie G.
I'm from Chicago, IL.
I try to take each day at a time and not worry about the future too much. It's helped me overcome a lot of obstacles in life, even though it doesn't seem like a lot. It seems really cheesy but I believe that everything works out for the best.

Alan Y

from Tianjin, China

Nobody can casually succeed, it comes from the through self-control and the own will.

157

7/2/16

Adam R.
Trenton IL

My dad died when I was little, and
it inspired me to be a carpenter like him.

Robert W.   Bloomington/
                             Southern IL
                             Seattle, Wash

I am inspired every day to be the best
person I can in spite of the people
that are not

AARON & Brooke D.   7-4-16
            Phoenix, AZ
    I find inspiration each day in the
eyes of my 2 year old son. I strive
to offer him my best version of myself
and the most opportunities I can offer
him.   LOVE
        Don - you are the coolest!!!

158

7/2/16	Nothing great was ever acheived without enthusiasm.
	Ralph Waldo Emerson
	ashley Benson, from $6 live in ATL

7/2/16	Everything happens for a reason.

7/2/16	YoLO - Butt

7/2/16	Live enjoy day like its your last!
	fun

7/2/16	Law of attraction !!
	Feel it as real !!
	—Angella St. Louis MO.

7/4/16

When life tells you, you can't or it will not happen. Keep pursing, push harder, fight harder, and never give up. For what you fight the most for is what makes you the happiest. Joe W.

7/4/16

No matter what happens in life, wake up every morning and be thankful for the one God gave you

Libby M.

160

7-4-16

'Always go with your gut feeling. I moved back from Colorado and two weeks later I got to meet the man I feel in love with. I had no idea back in September that thats why I was moving back, but I know thats why I moved back. Life takes you down so many different paths, but you always end up where you are meant to be. I absolutely, without a doubt, believe that. Have faith and trust things will work out just the way they are meant to.

—Lily

7/5/16

Nicole G.
University City
MO

The smallest issues used
to bother me.
My husband was diagnosed
with stage 4 throat cancer
16 months ago. He's in
remission now. Miracles
do happen.
You bet I no longer sweat
the small stuff and we
live each day on purpose.

Get Knocked Down 99 times
Get up 100 times

9/20
ACAN
T.

GREATNESS IS PREDICATED ON CONSISTENTLY
DOING THINGS OTHERS CAN'T OR WON'T DO. SIMPLY
PUT, SUCCESS IS NOT ABOUT BEING BRILLIANT, IT
IS ABOUT BEING CONSISTENT.

162

Barry B████ July 5, 2016
I grew up in St. Louis. My parents attended
Cleveland NJROTC Academy. That inspired me to
participated in JROTC. This ultimately led me to graduating
from West Point.
St. Louis, Mo — Kansas City, Mo — Monmouth, NJ —
West Point, NY — Fort Bragg, NC

Valerie C████ 5 July 2016
    In may of 2009 I enlisted in the US Army
as a medic. Upon graduation from AIT
my commander recommended I apply
to West Point -- at west point I worked with &
was in charge of the Sexual Harrassment & Assault
Program helping survivors & educating the corps of
cadets on impacts & realities so they could better
lead their soldiers. That company commander that
gave me my recommendation & pushed me changed everything
 Chaska MN — chatfield MN — Ft Sill OK —
Ft Sam Houston TX — Ft Stewart GA — West Point NY
— Ft Lee, VA

     ✗✗

Peter - St. Louis
- I am inspired by climbing mountains.
I climbed Mt Rainier a few years
ago and faced fear, exhaustion and
pain in a successful bid for the
summit. It taught me perseverance,
self reliance, and the power of
tackling an audacious goal one
step at a time.

Jamin - Ballwin
Lately, cooking has inspired me. Growing
up with a gourmet chef for a mother
it's something I've missed as a single
adult who never acquired the skill.
But if you just jump in and start
simple, it's not as difficult as you
might think. My favorite meal to
make? Quiche. Remarkably quick
to prepare and incredibly comforting.

7/5/16

Sujith, Maryland Heights.

I like to draw inspiration from several people
& events that I come across in my daily life. A good
gesture inspires me, a good smile inspires me, good attitude
inspires me.

I stay away from my family now for work. Thinking
about family inspires me — to go on and on, doing my
bit to make sure that I care enough for them.

My 1 year old son inspires me, to work hard and
get back to being with him.

It is rare to find people who really want to
inspire others, help others, nowadays. I like the intent
of your initiative, you inspire me! God Bless!

Cheers!

7/6/16 David, Chesterfield

I enjoy making things happen. The ability
to breakdown complex items into smaller manageable
chunks allows us to see what we thought we couldn't
achieve into something we can.

165

7/6/16   Abby / Kirkwood

try to find something
positive in each day even
if it's harder to find
something positive some
days because it well be better
in the end.

7/7/16

If I can smile at someone and they smile back at me, I have no reason not to be happy. - Ross, St. Louis

Today I'm in a "Pissy" mood & don't want to bring others down by writing something negative. I don't like it when someone dumps on me so I won't do it to others! Thanks for letting me vent to you.
~ Rebecca   Ste. Geneviève & now
              South City St. Louis

July 7, 2016

Every day I wake up I ask the question, what can I do to be a better person, achieve a better goal then the day before. I never really answer the question, although I do live by my own motto; No matter what life may bring you through, even if its not of your likings, there will always be a brighter and better day then tomorrow. Stay humble, stay studious, and stay kind. Love all.

Scott = Duke"

Joe G.   (Terminal Supervisor   Transport)

The military was one of the
greatest things that has happened
to me. On a mission in Iraq
I jumped out of a plane and
landed wrong and pinched
my nerve in my spine. I was
paralyzed from the waist down
by the grace of God and hard work
I am walking. The military
taught me strength and perseverance

Meeting Holocaust survivor IRENE BUTTER and hearing her teach school children about her experiences as a child in Berlin, and Amsterdam where she and her sister befriended Anne Frank ... they later saw her shortly before her death in the concentration camp where her family was imprisoned. Her story of survival and the importance of ~~teaching about~~ speaking out against injustice has ~~encouraged~~ motivated me to work ~~for~~ for social justice.

Meeting Dr. Billy Taylor – Mich

Meeting Dr. Billy Taylor, U of Michigan running back / All American (1968-7 who became addicted to drugs and alcohol after school + ended up ~~major~~ ~~and~~ homeless and imprisoned. He sobered up, completed his degree and now runs a drug + alcohol rehab center in Detroit.

Elena

Be
Happy !

Russia Rules

Nizhny

Novgorod

Learn Russian !

Love Russians !!!

My grandparents are the most inspirational people I know. They are both 90 years old and have seen a lot in their lives. They grew up during a hard time — where many people were treated unfairly. They were raised to treat everyone with respect and ~~kindness~~ kindness. They also have the most admirable relationship. Married for 70 years! They have impacted my life in more ways than they will ever ~~come~~ know! ~~& the love~~

I look to them for inspiration and motivation on everything from love, career advice, friendship, anything! I'm very grateful to have them in my life!

My relationship with God has been
a constant source of strength and hope,
I've been a Christ follower for all of my life.
In junior high I developed a relationship
with Jesus.

AA STL

LIFE - IT'S THAT SIMPLE
SHAWN M. MC.   - ST. LOUIS, MO

"You do not have to be good. You only
have to let the soft animal of your
body love what it loves." - Mary Oliver
L Lizzie M., St. Luis

~~~~~~ I found that I'm most motivated
by my friend's success and accomplishments - they
constantly push me to do better in my life and strive
for excellence - Harry P   STL

With the help of G-d all things
are possible; Trust in G-d's kindness
Jason

173

Joining The United States Army at 17 years
old to remove myself from a hard upraising
and giving me the foundation I have today —
making positive steps forward every day.

Chance @ Memphis

Being a first-born mexican American
w/a Dad who went through hell 7fold
just to give me an opportunity he could
only dream of. He saw his Dad get killed
in front of him at age 12 and had to emigrate
to the U.S. at age 16 to support his 8 sibling
family. He died when I was in the Navy
at age 19. I never forget him he truly
led by example I am 34 yrs old now.
And I make my money w/ my brains like
he always wanted me to. I miss him
dearly.

Anonymous

174

My sister just had her baby! —Bree C
St. Louis, MO.

My godmother Cindy has shown me what it takes to be an independent women in this society. The year I lost my mother, I am 22 years old... an adult. She taught me how to take care of myself under the circumstances. She showed me that it wasn't my fault. it wasn't anyones fault. She taught me that life is truly not easy for anyone we all go through things, but no matter what you keep going. Even when you angry, and even when you want to give up; you dont. She taught me that no matter what you can find the way.

Nicole

St. Louis

7/9/16

Christopher A ....com

I'm an artist, LoL

Ali McC
veterans are assets
The mission continues #CharlieMike
alillie.mcchng@gmail.com

I had the opportunity to spend a day working w/ mentally handicapped children. They showed such positivity & smiled for everything. they appreciate the bare minimum

-Jake J
Chicago IL

177

Matt S.

The Love Ive shared is
the Love Ive recieved.
Live,
Learn,
Love,
Drink Beer.

help me Im going to be
me murdered

murdered

GO CUBS

- Charlie S

I love my family especially my aunts and nephews. They give me a reason to exist and set a good example. I want to [be?] a solid example for [being?] out. I [learn?] ... than ... the world ... [loving?] + caring and accepting ... want everyone in my family to ... [love?] ... and set the example ... a loving, caring person ... not just them in my family but ... loving and accepting, good caring to all + everyone ... been everyone and everyone should accept ... everyone

Jessa- Newton IL.

My husband Kyle,

Is the most inspirational
person I know, he keeps me
going. We have 2 jobs its rough,
marrige is not easy. Especially with
2 children at home we try to
find time to me together but its
rough. We love each other
so much. I have never been
happier. My life is amazing,
thanks for the support.

Frank, Kansas City

I could not have gone to college with the quick help from to STL AIA. They loaned me money to start college and it made the difference in my life. Owe my architectural career to the AIA. Have set up two scholarship for students since

Beth E   7/11/2016
Columbia, MO
   My Biggest motivation in my life has
been my move to Columbia, MO from
Detroit. The lifestyle in Columbia has
been extremely active. It has motivated myself
my husband, and my two daughters to
take up running and hiking. Being health
is a priority in our lives everyday.

7/11/16

Michelle
St. Louis, MO

My son motivates me to be
a better person everyday.
I strive to be someone who
he is proud of. Through my
words, actions and love I
try to be a good example
and role model.

Milinda   7/12/16
Los Angeles

Don't be afraid of fear. Face it head
on. And say "Yes. I can"

The best thing in life is
self love. Teaching our children
this will change the world.
Self love must also be   Angela
combined with a humble spirit. Ft Myers

Jon (St. Louis)
Don't be afraid to be yourself,
be wierd, be bad,... be what you aont,
No one can make you change unless
you let them, so don't let them ☺

The best inspiration for my was my physical educational teacher. He was always the first who started person who encouraged other people to be mindful, help each other and make the world better place. His best quote was "there is a lot of sun for everybody". He was so influential because he was always the first one who started to help, clean rubish from streets or just bought a bunch of bananas and gave He to all my friends with words "I am giving you a smile". This person touched my heaulth and hopefully influenced the way I behave.

MATOUŠ, CZECH REPUBLIC

7/14/16

Kristina
San Franciso, CA

What most motivates me is my family. I want to make them proud and help support them, as they supported me. And my husband! His unconditional love keeps me going!

184

7/12/16

~~"Don't take guidance lig~~

"Don't take guidance lightly, or else
you will never find your way"
    — Johnathan
    — Scottsdale, AZ

Being kind to people will never make you unhappy but hate will breed hate.
Also everything is always going to work out okay whoever or whatever you lose.

Susan . C ☺ London

Recently my wife supported me through a medical process. While husbands and wifes are suppose to be there for each other, this event reminded me just how much she cares for me and will always be there for me

Sean D.   Denver

I am just impressed by the human spirit and the resillance that people have against life circumstances. My little brother died a few years ago and I thought that I just did not have the will to carry on. However through my travels I have meet many people that have given me the strength to use that loss to help others.

Terrieu-Atlanta

186

I found the following quote inspirational so I shared it with my adult children

— "Excellence will overcome obstacles"

— Roscoe Brown Tus ,, e Airman

I am not sure who said this first, but it has been an inspiration and motivation to me:

You will lose 100% of the shots you didn't take.

Kamil - -, Istanbul Turkey

I met a woman while I was in high school that was an engineer. She told me that I could do whatever I could dream. I set my sights on an engineering degree and have worked towards supporting + empowering other women in this field of work.   —Suzanna (Nashville, TN)

"Think of where you want to end up - and don't start there." I was unhappy @ a dead end job and not sure where I wanted my life to end up. I decided to pack up my life and move to an unknown city to start a job that made less money but gave me the opportunity to travel the world and meet people from all walks of life. It was the most terrifying but rewarding thing in my life. If it doesn't scare you - you're not taking a big enough risk. Life is too short to not go after your dreams - you may have to make sacrifices - but you owe it to yourself to try.
                    —Marianne (Tampa, FL / St. Louis, MO)

Andrea

Energy Flows Where Attention Goes.
~ From Yoga Teacher

TODD FROM PHOENIX
WHAT YOU REFIST PERSISTS

(Debbie) I live in chaos
every trying to relive in
free radicals

You can't control how the wind
blows, but you can control how
you set your sails

Kahe   7/12/16
Chicago!   Do what makes you happy because your happiness
(but went   shines through your actions... and who knows what/
to Wash.)   who you will help inspire to be the best version of themselves

                                                        7/12/16

            Don't judge others by their worst examples
Melanie   while judging yourself at your best intentions.
Chicago   Keep an open mind and an open heart, kindness
            and love will always trump fear and hatred.

189

Cierra - St. Louis, MO   7/13/16

What motivates me?
I would have to say my parents motivate me.
~~[scribbled out text]~~
~~[scribbled out text]~~

My parents have been together for 35 yrs. They
were high school sweethearts. Having 2 out of 4
children by the age of 19 & 20, they were
able to overcome being teenage parents & make
a way for their children. Having the other
2 later in life by the age of 29/30 they
were home owners, living middle class &
able to provide for & make a way for their
family. They motivate me to let nothing
stop me from doing what I want to do w/
my life. They let me know & any roadblock
is just temporary & can be gone through.
They are my biggest motivators & my
biggest rolemodels. They make me believe
that anything can be accomplished as long
as I don't give up.

190

Patrick   7/13
St. Louis, MO

What Motivates Me?
My Wife and my family to come...
We are six months pregnant with our
first child... a boy. I want to provide
for them, love them, and give them
my all. They deserve the best version
of myself. I hope to never let them down,
but to inspire them like they inspire
me.

7/13/16   Talking with people day to day
about a wide variety of topics
and hearing how they overcome
their unique issues/problems inspires
me.   I share my life's trials
and tribulations and how I
have overcome them as well.
It is my hope that I inspire
people that hear how I have
dealt with my issues in life.
Our world would be a better
place if we had more conversation
and less altercation.
Peace Out   Springfield, MO

191

7/13/16

This is your one only life. Here, in the body you are in now, is all you have. Commit to it.

Amber, Oakland, CA

I've been lucky enough to work for a great family owned company where we work hard and they reward hard work and they have given me a great opportunity in life to live out my dreams.

Mike, Raleigh NC

I always wanted to go abroad and study and fulfill my dreams and experience different pattern of classes and courses. After making so much of effort, I made my way to U.S.A. and I completed my Master from University of Central Missouri. I feel myself quite lucky.

Ankush, India (Jabalp

7-26-16

Embrace technology & be the change you want in the world!

Sara
Fond du lac, WI

192

AMIT

People have The power to heal or to hurt. I believe in making people feel good about themselves. This is one thing that they will always remember about you. What that inspired me carry on with my thought process is because of the people I have met who have selflessly helped or offered help to me. There have been times when I was depressed and even angry when some one deliberately hurt me or even someone else. Then some times on the same day there was an act of kindness. It seems like a mystery when the same person is able to do two polarizing things. I hope to keep learning and grow and help when I am able to just like others have done the same for me.

7/19/14 I was fortunate enough to have a strong faith network and a very supportive wife who stood by my side when I lost my job on 2 seperate occasions. It is our faith, family & friends who are there to prop us up, support us and be there for us to get us thru adversities. Trust in all 3 and make sure when given the opportunity, that you return the favor. Joe H St. Louis. Mo

194

Assane _____ ___, from Dakar, Senegal (West Africa)

So all my life I always dreamed to become a soccer player and I never gave up on that dream. At the age of 13 being in my country and playing in an academy I had the chance to be recruited to go finish my formation in France but my mom was against that idea, for her studies always came first and she always thought that a terrible injury before becoming pro might happen to me. But I never gave up and kept training hard and doing my best. Finally 1 years ago I got recruited by Saint Louis University to come study with a and play soccer for them. My mom accepted and here I am now in Saint Louis playing for an NCAA D1 team and giving my best to be drafted by a MLS Team and achieve great. So just never give up and you will always find the way to get to where you want to.

195

My Mom is the most influental person in my life. My parents got divorced when I was young and even though my father was not a part of my life my mom made up for it. She made me the Man I am today

Jimmy   Fort Worth TX

I have no physicians in my immediate family. Despite that, my mother and father gave me every opportunity to pursue my early aspiration of becoming a doctor. Now only three years away from achieving that goal, I can't put a value on the sacrifices that they made for me everyday growing up. Personal motivation is key for fulfilling one's goals, but a strong support network should never be taken for granted

Michael M, Orange County, CA

Music is the cure to my heartaches. Its the perfect match for my soul, uplifting. Music eases pain without trying, gives you a different outlook on life, perception. Music saved my life. Peace + Love

-Amber, Chicago
7/21/16

My brother Robbie was born with severe disabilities. He has trouble walking well and struggles with social skills. Next week he is going to college, and has graduated high school by officially passing the state exam designed for kids of full ability.

-Chris, Boston

whenever I need a source of motivation, I look straight up. What I love most is thinking about how insignificant I really am. I think about all of the people in airplanes above me that never would even know that I existed. When I need to get that extra bit of help to accomplish a task, it relieves me to know that whatever I do, it isn't the end of anything.

Sam, Boston Hills

197

Ryan M. _ (Chesterfield)

I was really close with my grandpa and shared everything with him. He was everything to me, my best friend, father figure and mentor. He helped me along the through times, cracked jokes with me, and made me feel like I had a spot in this world even when I didn't. He taught me that you should keep working hard and be everyone's friend cause they might be able to help you. He taught me to keep fighting for the one you love even when you're battling cancer. He was all I had and I don't want to let him down. He inspired me to be the best me and to work for what I believed I deserve.

7-20-16   Les
                            Chicago
    Always do the right thing.
That's what I've learned in life
that will make you the happiest.
Humans are unique. They don't
just act. They know the difference
between right and wrong. We shouldn't
overthink our decisions in life. We
should simple always do the
    Right thing.

If life gives you lemons, control
what you can control and be a winner.
Focus on winning at what you can
control and in time you will become a
champion. The more persistent you we
and the more you practice, the "luckier"
you will become.
7-20-16   RAM   Austin

199

"LIVE FOR THE MOMENT"
— Doc
stl

As I get older I realize that I need to trust my gut more. I find more & more that if I trusted my gut about people, situations, ideas, I'd be just fine.

So trust your gut!

Chris
St Louis, MO

Samantha   Memphis TN
My family, especially my younger brother
motivate me to be a better person &
example especially when it comes to my
spiritual journey. My church & the community
of friendship there also inspires me to be the
best christian I can be & be a light in this
dark world.

Anoup   St. Louis

During Tsunami tragedy in India, I get to visit
those places and participated in the relief projects.
It was It was my first experience and the whole
scene was tragic — but I have seen lot of good
people there helping others — It was a big
inspiration to see the good side of humanity,
helping the people in need.

201

7/25/16   Greg F.   TWP New Jersey

My FAMILY IS my INSPIRATION.
That BEINg SAID, my advice IS To
TALK To people, Put DOWN YOUR cell phone
and TALK To People. Communication
IS Key. GIVE People A chance. You may
Be surprised & pleased with what People
have to say.

202

7/26 Nealette Houston, TX. in St. Louis for
      Katherine Dunham Technique Seminar.
      I've been inspired by people again.
      The ~~helpful~~ hospitality + spirit of
      the people is still alive - Even though
      some parts of the city appears to be
      wiped out. There's still hope here.

7/26   Elena G. , _____ Queens, NYC
          What inspires me is the reassurance & idea that
      you can begin again at every moment. Every second,
      with every breath you get an opportunity to try something
      differently or again → or to completely start over.
          What inspires me is discovering and exploring the
      intelligence and capability of the human body to evolve,
      to store personal & generational memories, and to
      release, restore, and heal → no matter what so-called
      "age."
          What inspires me is ~~the~~ being around people
      who are living their true life purpose, unabashedly.

7/26   Truth = Only Shared Whole
       "Trade" is the fragmented imitation of a thief. It
       destroys the sharing of truth, leads to mental
       and spiritual Death. -Le'Andre

203

7/26/16

Life is short. Enjoy every day. Explore —
Participate, contribute, be happy —
share your knowledge, love, Be open,
be fair, listen, dream, be humble,
be gracious, — care!

Denise and Sue St. Louis

7/26/16   Mark W. - Norfolk, VA → St. Louis, MO

Remember that you are unique. You're one of
a kind. Keep that thought and keep in mind
that everyone else is unique too. Spread love
and cherish the love that is given to you. Last
thing is to laugh as much as possible. That always
makes things better. ☺

I never dreamed of living in St. Louis.
I grew up in KC hating this city - you can
thank the '85 World Series for that. But
we moved into a wonderful neighborhood in South City
and I've fallen in love with the city over time, looking
past its faults & appreciating the positives - the people
of this city.
                    - W

A positive effect on my life is my mom.
I lost my dad at a young age but through
everything has kept me stable. I know she
works hard for me everyday and soon I
will be able to pay her back.

Antwan
St. Louis

9/1/16

FRANK — ST LOUIS

Inspiration of my ~~map~~ Martial Arts
instructors guided my life in dedication, dvlpmnt.
of busines, Knowldge of drive to better myself
and have become a motivational sales trainer

9/2/16   D.W. — ~~ST. LOUIS~~ TALLAHASSEE

5th HARMONY TOUR DRIVER. Im lucky
to be involved in music, it gives people
joy. I get to meet cool and intresting
people all over USA + CAN. I miss my
dog, Frankie. CANT WAIT to see my
family + Friends at home. Go NOLES!

Insert
Image
of Bey. | Beyoncé Formation Tour is
amazing! Make sure you see
her in your lifetime!

IGOR — BOULDER, CO (ZAGREB, CROATIA)

Running gives me time off from daily activities ... Getting
on the trail with sound of nature and your own steps
is peaceful ... TRY it sometimes.

Keishae   St Louis - Chicago

Going to school on a full ride scholarship has made me more
aware of the blessings to come in my adult years Also
being away from home allows me to miss it and be
able to bring something back when I do return

Sam   y. Lanzhou, China
Work hard doesn't assure a success, but
give up will definitely lead to failure

Jeff   Beijing — Columbus Ohio

Focus your time & energy and you will
have a shot at accomplishments. It takes
much work to learn to focus at all times,
but the time you save from worrying and
gossiping will prove to be of great value.
Also Aim higher if you want to go further

I would say my inspiration would be my teacher who was blind. I was really amazed how he could do all of those things, I mean how he could recognise us just with our voices. He always said no matter what always move on.

→ OM BHGTWAL
ॐ भट्टवाल
From NEPAL

Inspiration to me is my mom and her motivations. Because she taught me never to give up.
नमस्ते (Namaste) it means greeting hello
Chhaya K.C.
छाया के.सी
Nepal.

I have ~~come across~~ met a lot of people and had a lot of experiences which have inspired me and shaped my life, but one interaction stands out.

I was conducting a household health survey in a Karachi slum, when I ended up surveying a house full of children mature beyond their years, managing everything like grown-ups and wonderfully optimistic on their outlook on life. The catch? They had hearing and vision impaired parents, and they all had some degree of sense impairment.

I have found it difficult to be ungrateful since.

SAAD. 5,
Karachi, Pakistan

Love. When we fight it we lose. From a
young age. Give love share love and you will
change your world and everyone around you.

Rob W.

Do what makes you happy! Let your
heart be happy! Let your heart be
be brave! ♡ ♡ ♡♡ Jamie - St. Louis
♡

Kevin - Princeton - NJ
Alaska was the most ~~beautiful~~ beautiful place
I have ever been. Any place I looked was a view
to be seen. Never before was I so off the grid and
in the wild. I have always ~~contrasted~~ contrasted this
trip with life back east, bustling NYC vs the jagged
peak of Mt. Mckinley.

Chloe - Boston
The man at chipotle gave me a free
burrito bowl because he heard me complaining about guy troubles
to my friend. he said "its free have a good day beautiful"
when I went to pay and it made me happy

Nuala - Boston
coming back to school and seeing all my
friends I missed over the summer.

Lina - Colombia.

I have been in ~~XXXX~~ USA for almost 1 year, I get married and i alredy traver to 14 states in USA and i want to finish here my career like a dentist and adopt a dog and all of this just in nex year.

Lisa - St. Louis

"My crown is in my heart, not on my head; not decked with diamonds and Indian stones, not to be seen; my crown is called content, a crown it is that seldom kings enjoy."
William Shakespeare

Favorite: Brasserie, Olio, Olive + Oak
Restaurants

Ahmed from Morocco, 22 years old
Casablanca (and Madrid)

The ~~very~~ most inspirational person for
me is my grandfather. As he started
his life without money and he could
offer me the comfortable life that I have
now. He's a self made man
that proved me that I could succeed
also. Thanks to him, I am currently
in Saint Louis studying to be
as successful as him. Hopefully he's
been watching everything since his death.

Mrs Jalila and Mr Abdelmajd
Morocco, Casablanca.

Nous sommes marocains. Nous
venons du Maroc, de Casablanca
parents de trois garçons. Nous
sommes venus installer notre troisieme
fils Ahmed a Saint Louis pour
terminer son bachelor a SLU
Cette experience a été l'une des plus
positives de notre vie car elle nous
a permis de rencontrer des personnes
très ouvertes aux autres, une popula
tion multiculturelle qui semble
avoir depassé certains prejuge, qui
existent encore dans d'autre regions
du monde et cela est très agrea
ble.

We are Moroccans, We came from
Morocco, Casablanca, parents of 3 children.
We came here to have our son settled
in Saint Louis to get his bachelor degree
in SW. This experience has been very
positive in our life as it gave us
the opportunity to open ourselves to
the others, a population which
is multicultural which is over
stereotypes that exists in other regions
of the world and that is super good.

215

Taylor - St. Louis

I experience a lot of things in my field of Nursing. There are a lot of things that have made a difference in my life, but there is one story that has stuck with me through everything. While in nursing school, I met a young 8-year-old girl struggling with cancer. I was fortunate enough to spend five days of clinical with her. Some days she wanted to play with others in the playroom - other days when she was feeling sicker we would color in her room. Listening to her talk about chemotherapy and treatments was very hard to hear, yet she spoke with such hope and determination to beat anything thrown at her. Her outlook and positivity on life was so inspirational to me and made me change how I feel about my own outlook. This girl, though so young and so sick, had the best attitude and I admired her so much for that. I never found out what happened to her but she did make a profound impact on my life.

Justin – Texas

As a physician, I have been fortunate enough to experience many positive experience in my field of work. Probably the most privledged I have been is in sharing end of life with patient's family and friends. Though very sad, it is an essential part of life which I am fortunate enough to experience so up close and personal. During these moments, I am more fully aware of how important the special people are to me and remember how fragile life really is. ~~is and~~

VAIBHAV,

My biggest motivation inspiration is my
father, My hero, he has helped during
My all tough times, & Even during very
tough situations where People hesitate to
share with father - But i did share &
i Just loved the way he responded
me back as friend, he helped me
to when I failed in my secondary Education.
when i failed in my love, when i have
fights to face tough situation with my
wife, when i failed finencially
Yes. Iam very Lucky to have him &
for any thing that i am now —
is all because of my Dad &
his frindly talles, motivational talles,
Boosting and..

Tony

My little Cousin Faith, —
Faith was 6, diagnosed with Ewings Sarcoma—
A Cancer in the spine. She fought, and beat
it. She inspired So many people and she always
had a smile. But. The cancer came back.
Childhood leukemia - This was no Joke —
She fought through a bone marrow Transplant
- a serious & life threatning procedure. IY went
good - She had to stay near the hospital in
Case anything happened. One day she run
a fever and had to go in. She was 9 at this

July 28, 2016

    I know it's hard to overcome anxiety depressions or any other adversities. I used to be very depressed and bored with my job, and I lost my grandmother after I came to the U.S. Actually things won't turn better if you only focus on your pains.

Yi

China

Teny T - continued
point - Unfortunately she never left.
going into an operation, her heart failed during
poep & she passed. She was awesome. She
was a true super hero. RIP Faith Hartzell.
Remember- ~~one~~ Always keep the faith.
When times are rough always look to
the positive. ~~The~~ Times get tough but it leads to
better things. ② Keep ~~your~~ your head up!!

just some encouraging words that have helped me accomplish magnificent things

Make a wish & put on your smile. Get ready to accomplish the incredible you can do whatever you set your mind & your heart to. Wear your ~~smile~~ smile and remember that you are capable of anything you imagine.

7/25/16 - 1 principal & 3 RN's
Group from Spfld, IL

life is about choices and consequences

You must be happy w/yourself before
    you can be happy w/life

yolo olan'

Nachos are great = life

Happiness may seem easy but you
    must be happy

HAVING BEEN SOME OF THE MOST IMPOVRESHED COMMUNITIES IN LATIN AMERICA, I CAN ALWAYS FIND MOTIVATION IN THE RESILIENCE OF PEOPLE. THE PEOPLE IN THESE COMMUNITIES ARE POOR IN MATERIAL GOODS BUT RICH IN LOVE & HOPE. DON'T LET YOUR MISFORTUNES KEEP YOU UNHAPPY. FIND HAPPINESS!

JOSE
AUSTIN, TX

A life changing experience I've had is getting a DWI. I thought it was terrible at the time. I dropped out of college to work to afford my legal fees. But Now, 6 years later I own my own home, will graduate college in December. And have had an unmeasurable amount of memories. All bc I was arrested that night and moved back to St. Louis. The message of this is sometimes terrible tragedies are blessings in disguise.

Life is full of choices &
Consequences

Always judge another by their situation
rather than their disposition.
Scott L. ~ Chicago, IL

No one of us is as strong as all of us.
—Jenna T., Chicago, IL

"All women should walk like
3 men are walking behind
them"
—Nina

7/30/16

My dad has been an alcholic for my entire life. He was very physically + emotionally + sexually abusive. I do not feel sorry for what I went through, he has made me stronger. My mom has been my saviour - she saved me and has been my mom + dad. He almost killed her which is so embarrasing. He is sad. I feel bad for people who don't appreciate life, I'm so grateful for my mom, she has made me who I am.

Good luck w/ your book :)
        Stacey - Waterloo, IA

224

My biggest motivation and enjoyment comes from my son. He's 14 months old and everyday I walk in the house from work he runs full speed to jump into my arms. Then shows me his toys. It's almost as if its scripted from a movie, and by far the best part of my day!

Devin
St. Louis
8-1-16

Live everyday to the fullest and be grateful for everything!

Suzy
St. Louis
8-2-16

Tabitha H_____.
from: St. Louis, MO
One my biggest inspiration is my little
girls and my husband. They motivate me
to be a better person. I want them to know
if I can do it, they can do it too.

8/3/16
Michelle K_____ ___ ― St. Louis MO
As a believer in Christ, I can
say that I have personally
experienced His Grace, Mercy
& Favor. I have Sooooooo
many testimonies... But I'll
Share one that personally touches
my heart the most.
    At 1 point I was contemplating
leaving my husband because he was
not concerned w/ my or our
kids feelings AT ALL!!
    I prayed for him, our marriage
our home, our family - all while
asking the Lord to give me the patience
to deal w/ everything!!
    To make a long Story short →

Traveling around with family
& friends. Danielle S.   - Arlington WA

Being able to care a fun "business trip" & girls trip
with my long time friends. The business is
yunique cosmetics. - Kathleen woods
- Everett WA

Being a mom and mentor to
children. Living a happy healthy
life full of love.
                              Dawn M.
                        Granite Falls, WA

BRITTANY FROM ST. LOUIS MISSOURI,

~~Oh~~ ~~Rafe~~

ABOUT 4 yrs AGO I WAS SHOT BY AN
UNKNOWN SHOOTER RANDOMLY. I LIVED, IN
SO MANY ~~WAYS~~ WAYS I'm AFFECTED BY
THIS. THIS MAJOR EVENT TOUCHED ME IN
SO MANY WAYS THAT iT MOTIVATES ME
TO PUSH MY DREAMS. MY LIFE WAS
SPARED FOR SO MANY REASONS, I'm
DETERMINED TO KNOW.

Elana, Berkeley CA
My kids inspire me every day. Even on days when
I am at my least patient - they are at their
most patient. And ~~even~~ on days when they are
facing new challenges - they inspire me. Its a
wonderful thing to see the world through their eyes.

228

Peggy, St. Louis 8/4/16

The best thing that I ever happened
to me was being the result of
my parents. Everything since then
is because of them.
They are funny and shrewd and
smart and active and they love
me and my husband and my dog - even
my in laws.
I'm happy to know them and love
them and I hope to be half as
great as they are, when I'm
their age.

Peter / Katie   St. Peter, MN

Inklings is a great idea. Don't
have much to add at this point
Short Ride. But hope your Book
   is a success.
"Sometimes you've gotta work a little to be
a ot baller."
                    Katie St. Peter, MN

If you and when you fail,
be damned sure it wasn't because
you didn't try hard enough!

A little over a year ago I decided to apply for business school. Some people right away told me I'd be able to get in. Most just opened their eyes and wished me good luck, and half of them kindly told me it was a longshot and that I was better off saving my money. Today I finished my first week as an MBA student at Washington University in St Louis with a full ride scholarship. Trust yourself, you really are THAT GOOD!

Roberto C. O____, Puerto Rico
August 5, 2016

Brenna from Kansas City

Some of the best deasions you make
will be deciding to say no.
Knowing when to leave a job,
relationship, etc. is always hard
but sometimes you can't move
forward without leaving something
behind, and finding something even
better. Volunteer at Great Plains ~~Ad~~
Adoption Center. Kerah from Kansas City.

No Matter what, in the end,
everything will be okay, if
its not okay, its not the end.

~Maren, STL

Live for
plan for today
tommorow

~~Devin~~ in loving
of memory
danny Reed

20+ years of
Brain Cancer

Love

Devin

I'm an oncology nurse. I work nights. I was with my friends tonight but couldn't stop thinking about a patient I care about so I ~~was~~ pretended I was tired and left.

Kadi
Jerseyville, IL

Claire

Everyone has family problems. You can look at a family and think that they are perfect or that they just have first world problems but sometimes first world problems can be just as pressing on the mind as real problems. Yes... I'm middle class... Yes I had private school education my whole life but there are so many things people don't know. My father is an alcoholic. It has been pressing on me the whole summer to ignore it. I have anxiety. People think it is something to push off but it is not a promise. My brother has slow processing so he has been bullied his whole life. We seem like your typical keeping up with the Jones' but inside we are chaos and love and hope. Hope that someday we can all be grateful for the life we are given. I was an athlete, a leader of my student scholarship program. I am just a human who wants love in my family and a future that is comfortable. I hope I can have that someday despite my inability to have best friends or love. I hope that someday someone will love me.

♥ Claire St.Louis

Personally, music could
not inspire me any more.
Without music, I'm
nothing.

♡ Kelli
Lake Forest, IL

Don,

Thank you so much for the ride. I can't tell you how much it means to us. I wish you all the best in your future rides and hope that everyone treats you with the respect that you truly deserve. Thanks for everything.

Love,

Ryan + Tom

Today was a major stepping stone for me I started my job at a hospital something I always wanted. Despite all the trials & tribulations and near death experiences I manage to stay positive & keep my faith. Hopefully my new job is everything I expect it to be

By Ms Understood

Amber H saint Lous md

I've found in life that no matter what my perspective is, I am exactly where I'm supposed to be, doing exactly what I'm supposed to be doing. Therefore, it's of paramount importance to embrace the present!

~ Daniel
(Sax Player in Band) Slightly Stoopid
8/8/16

Hi!
  This is a great idea!! I'm new to STL
+ I'm going my first Cards game today!
I'm really loving it here so far. Everyone is so friendly + my dog is loving
Forest Park. I've met so many amazing
ppl since ween came to STL. Each driver is
so different + has great stories. Moving
across country alone is a scary thing
to do, but Missouri has been incredibly
welcoming. Sometimes you just need to
take a leap in life. You might land
somewhere amazing!

                    Kari
                    8/8/16

I thought I had everything until I had children. They are the joy of my life.

— James O.
San Antonio, TX

08/08/2016 — Ji — from Central Pennsylvania
As a transplant to STL for grad school (PhD
in biology), I have met many great people who
inspired me in ways that I cannot imagine.
I came to STL several years ago after spending
my most of years out on the East Coast, and knew
less than 5 people in not just STL, but Midwest
as a whole. Since then, I have met many friends,
colleagues, and overall felt very welcome. I went to
a wedding last year in Peoria (IL). I visited
Denver to see a guy I met via work here
(hopefully see you soon!) Overall, STL as a whole
has been the inspiration itself ——— and oh, Go
Cardinals!

Lauren - ballwin mo

the most positive thing that motivates
me is my children they are
amazing & inspirational

POSITIVE INFLUENCE ON MY LIFE WAS THE MILITARY. I WAS A ~~XXXXX~~ PARATROOPER IN THE 82ND AIRBORNE THIS CHANGED THE LIFE OF TROUBLED YOUTH FOREVER. I AM NOW A SUCCESSFUL FATHER OF 2 AMAZING CHILDREN.

CHRIS R_____
CELL 703 786 1855
HERNDON, VA

Most positive influence on my life has been my oldest brother. He has 15 years on me so I've always looked up to him, but the biggest influence he had was watching him make his dreams come true and never losing site of ~~xxxx~~ what ~~xxxx~~ matters most to him.

Olina B____
Atlanta, GA

"No fail, no know; he who creates that must start with enduring hardship — when he has done that, he may begin to look for the pleasure and profit that [ideas are] to bring."

      — Lucian

We are privileged to live in a free society that values creativity, artistic expression, autonomy, intellectual discovery and where self-discovery and transformation are only possible through *this*.

      — N.M., San Francisco, CA

Laura from New Orleans
    I lost my home in Katrina,
but 10 years later, I'm still
    living in NOLA, have a successful
career, and am about to get
married. Even though life
was really hard, in a just a
few short years, it got so
much better than before!

Area 0: (s inspire)
Meeting people of different backgrounds
and from different places has been
the most positive aspect of life.
It is always exciting to wake up
every morning and what people
and ideas I will meet /see /hear
during the day

I am always reminded that gratitude
is possible no matter your circumstances
— Brent

~~Took us 5 years before we were able to have kids~~

~~Took~~
Tried having kids for 5 years with no success, finally when hope was almost lost had a baby boy and ANOTHER one 18 months after. They are my world
- Anthony
Kirkwood, Mo

Paul, New York via England

Moving to St Louis has had a very
positive impact on my life. The
Town is very family focussed and the
pace is a little slower than NYC
so I get to spend a lot more time
with the wife + kids

Samantha
Philadelphia, PA

The biggest gift in my life has
been the opportunity to travel. I think experiencing
other communities, both domestic and abroad opens
your mind and heart and truely allows you
to connect with others.

Samantha
St. Louis, MO

I am most greatful for my
education. My education has
gave me the opportunity to travel,
meet people from different backgrounds,
and has opened my mind to a
different way of thinking. I am
greatful for my mentors that
have helped me along the
way!!

Never think your too young.
canse when I was 18 I hit
the clubs real Hard a partied
my ass off. I Ran out
everyone that was older than
me.
JORDAN
Milwaukee WI

I was top in my school and got
into good university, one of the best
in my country, then I started to feel
great about myself and the success
got into my head and then starting
my downfall. But soon I realized
and learnt a lesson, never think you
are top of the world.

"If the people around you are
happy, you will be happy"

Thanks
BHANU,
St. Louis, MO

Tiffany, Overland Park, ~~KS~~ KS

My ~~parents~~ family is from overseas ~~in~~ in Taiwan & my parents are first generation immigrants. What impresses me ~~even~~ even more though, is my grandpa, who moved to Taiwan from China as a soldier during the occupation. He stayed in Taiwan, worked odd jobs & built a life, did well enough to send two of three kids to America & help them get settled my homes of their own. I talk to him every day via Skype & he's still trucking on & living life @ the age of 84.

Laura / Chicago, IL

I always think its important to find strength
within. Never underestimate the power you
can have over your own life. Be true to
what you believe in and treat other people
the way you want to be treated.
Unkind, mean things come from places of
insecurity. avoid those places and allow
yourself to truly be happy.

Ronan, KC.
Moved from Ireland to US. It
really is land of opportunity if you work
at it.

Hard work ALWAYS pays off. If things are going wrong, don't blame yourself. Instead try accomplishing your goal a different way. Along the way, there will always be people smarter, richer, more accomplished, but that doesn't mean you are worth ~~anything~~ any less. I always thought that unless I was "naturally" gifted or ~~tota~~ talented, I cannot be successful. One failure doesn't define you or your life. There is always time to start again. Even if you fail for whatever reason, enjoy every part of life and view each failure as a learning experience!

- Shreya
  Chandler, AZ

257

Traveling around with my new fiancé has been very inspiring and comforting. The more we travel together — whether it's to Detroit or Jamaica, we make the most of our trips, learn more about each other, and meet interesting people.

William — Jersey City, NJ

I'm constantly inspired by my travels, no matter where, as I find that each new trip either teaches me something, or reminds me of something I've forgotten about myself. Being able to share my travels with the love of my life makes this even better. We are the best travel buddies and could easily backpack the world together if we wanted. Traveling together reminds me how much is out there to be explored.

Liz — Jersey City, NJ

258

With each day that passes, I become more & more grateful for the two wonderful people that I'm lucky enough to call my parents. They've given me everything that I have & every opportunity I could've possibly asked for but still keep finding ways to give. I can't wait until I am able to start giving back to them a fraction of what they deserve.

Autumn
Northern Virginia
just moved to St. Louis

What ever it is that you think
you want you will get it if you want
it bad enough.
PAUL FROM SANDIEGO

God is always us... that's what
Keeps me going and strong!

DESHA FROM
ST. LOUIS

The goodness in other people, the love of my family and
the certainty that there is much grace in the world.
Jara, Costa Rica

Lo más importante en mi vida son mis hijas.
Ellas me llenan mi corazón.
DINA, Costa Rica

I think we got born, only, with a bad package
the dead of your Mom, a sick time, poor Health,
problems.. so it's up to you to provoke as many good
moments as you can to make the difference, it is
up to you to make the balance positive! Make of every
moment a great one... the best! Daniel, costa rica

260

8/15/16

YOU CAN OR CAN'T — BOTH
ARE INSIDE YOU.

— CHRIS "SPIKE"
HAWAII

8-17-16
    Stuff happens, but ~~how~~ how a
person handles the "stuff" is
~~a~~ a measure of a person's
character.

Kevin & Anne
Chesterfield, MO.

261

The more you dance with crazy people,
the more you look crazy yourself.

-Joe, St. Louis

If you're looking for a graduate assistantship, don't sweat it. You will either connect with the prof or you won't. It's not ~~gra~~ about you, it's about ~~the~~ chemistry. Good luck! —Dora, SLU

Austin where being weird is in! Just don't come here
- Emon, Austin

THE MORE YOU CAN MAKE LAUGHTER PART OF YOUR DAILY LIFE, THE MORE YOU can~~stone~~, ~~the~~ and The more fun you will have doing it.
BBC, WASHINGTON, DC

May you be in
heaven, a half hour
before the devil
knows your dead.

An Irish Toast

Martha A.   Springfield, MO   8/19/16
What motivates me is to be the person that others enjoy
to learn and be around. To inspire, to make laugh, to be a
good friend, collegue. To make those that watch over me proud.

8-19-16

Monica H.
I AM MOTIVATED BY GRANDMOTHER AND THE
REMEMBANCE OF THE SACKIFICES SHE MADE
TO MAKE SURE I WOULD HAVE A CHANCE AT
A BETTER life.

Bailey C.

I got into the city police academy
and I'm going to kick ass ✝✝
love my friends!

~~Amy S.~~

~~I am motivated to love being active~~
because (next page)

Ally S.

Nobody picks their family... but if you're
lucky enough, you meet the people that
you were destined to have in your life,
and then they become forever friends.
That is what keeps me going. They are
the reason I am who I am. ~~Everybody~~
I'm in love with my friends.

Christy M.
i guess if i could share any one thought
it would be to just love first. don't be
so quick to judge, or hate, ~~anyone~~ or compare...
just love, and listen.

Leah G.

Don't be so quick to judge. You have NO
idea what anyone has undergone. I
was raped when I was 17. I rarely to never
talk about it. People are rude & hurtful.
I have tried to kill myself. My friends
I met in college (not in high school who were
there for the rape) have kept me alive.
I am grateful for their love & support.
Find your true friends & hold them close.
even if its only 3 or 4.   -STL

Mare
finaly picked a major to do and a College to go to.
Marie - Columbia mo.

Leo = I adopted 2 beautiful
daughters from Russia in 2001,
It changed my life for
better - Best Decision I
ever made.
    Heart Body & Soul
        Columbia, Mo
        Deborah   y—

One time in elementary school, I pooped my
pants, and when I told the teacher about it,
all the other kids overheard and laughed at me.
That's the day I learned not to share my shit
with anyone.
        Michael H.

Enjoy the small things - your favorite flavor of ice
cream, the smell of wind in the fall, a strangers smile,
whatever it is, that's where hapiness comes from

Keith – St. Louis
Just keep swimming

It's important to feel connected to the world
around you. The most important moments of my life so far are
when I'm sharing my life, my hugs, my dreams with my family,
my best friends, or with complete strangers. Any time
there's an opportunity to be together with thousands of
people at one place, whether it's a concert, sporting event,
or rally, just go. It's worth it.
— Connor K.   St. Louis, MO

If you choose not to Decide you
still have made a choice
~~Saint~~ ~~Lewis~~ St Louis MO

I enjoyed taking uber to Kobe steakhouse
of japan at the top at westport with my
daughter and back

Listen to ~~the only~~ advice that is given to you. You may think that you have the answers, but you do not.

-Gabe S.C, ho

Basel, Palestine

Don't give up, don't stop. This one step
could be the one that leeds you to
achieve your goal. I almost gave up on
my university cause it was taking me
forever to finish and graduate. I pushed
myself and desided that it was about time
take a breake from doing both "work and
collage" and focuse on my studies. So after
being in and out, droping semesters for work
and taking a semester of studying, which took
over 8 years. It was time to get my
degree. Last year I got all As.
        Graduated, worked in my field and was
Respected more for the degree. Worked in a play,
a show, and Sesame Street in one year.
"Directing Crew and production" after that got
an interview in a TV channel with double the
salary of most people that were
working there.
            again don't give up and don't
stop, one step makes a big difference.

He also told me he owns a
    dinet called "   "
              on Natural Bridge Rd

269

This time in our lives is ridden with racism & we think every generation hates the other. This time in our country's history will forever remain as a fundamental stepping stone into the future. The comparison of the "Walk on Selma" to the "Black Lives Matter" movement will forever change the landscape of the racial tension that has been created in the last decade (2006-2016). The tragedies that have happened recently involving law enforcement have been a poor demonstration of patriotism and respect. The men & women that wear the badge have a truly thankless job & deserve the most respect of any person to date. May God bless this country & the men & women who defend this wonderful country. God bless the USA.

We Love ~~God!~~
~~God!~~
God!

Lauren
Webster Groves

Hello Friend,

Have fun tonight!
Always remember
the golden rule!
Treat everyone how
you want to be
treated.

And visit

National Rules!,

Recently got back from a backpacking trip w/ 50 other freshmen called "WP" or Wilderness Project w/ Wash U. The trip was fun but the true awesomeness came off trail when we were all hanging out and shering ~~everyone~~ everyone's personal stories. I was amazing to see how real of people everyone actually is, how much everyone has gone through. Having known these other students for only about a week it's mind blowing to compare the way I view them before and after hearing all these people's stories. Every human has a story. Every human has lived a life full of amazingly positive and negative experiences. ~~but all together~~ and that was an awesome realization.

Giles Massachusetts

BE GOOD.

ARE YOU KIND?

8/29/16

I would say one of, if not the most positive impact in my life would be my freshman theology teacher. The vast amounts of knowledge and life-lessons I have learned from him about faith, people, and the world around me have been helpful to my life in many ways. This has led to an increase in faith life, which for me is one of the most important parts of life. Overall I am very thankful for the wisdom he has granted me, and am also thankful for this oppurtihity to share.

        -Miles, St. Louis MO

I have been blessed with a great life this far. I have a Beautful wife and 3 amazing kids. Even though we don't struggle with alot of issues the rest of the world may, we still have our challeges. The only things that keeps me moving forward is knowing that this world is temporary and my heavenly father has a plan for me regardless what the future holds for me and my family.

        On our way to the Airport to leave to head back to them and then off to Germany

        - Jordan, US Air Force
           Omaha, NE - via Detroit

Failure is more enlightening than success.

        —J.E. New Orleans.
          "Jay Bridges"

Entropy is a fundemental part of the universe.
It is chaos, change. Change drives you to
grow, to succeed, to improve. You can and will
always adapt to whatever comes at you. So
whenever you feel lost, just know that
you're meant to keep going, that the
universe wants you to succeed.
        —Neel
          San Francisco

What motivates me is the ability to help others and make a difference in the world. My goal in life is to be able to alleviate the suffering of others throughout the course of my life, in any way I can.

— Ty F , St. Louis

Never be afraid to be different.
One of my favorite quotes I found on a juice pouch... it said "be yourself because everyone else is already taken."

—Cienna
Carmel, IN

A couple of weeks ago I lost someone really ~~so~~ important to me. for awhile I was lost in my life, I didn't want ~~to~~ to eat, go out or Anything. One day I ~~told~~ told myself I could do it, so I can do it. If life doesn't ~~go~~ stop, why should I stop? keep it moving!

—Ulises
Phx ~ Az

277

When I got heartbroken by a girl I was so hurt that
I didn't do nothing or talk to anybody for a long time
and I was so upet but I learn that you shouldn't dwell
on a person that never cared. So I got a person who
did" -J DeUntez C.   ;/ Tez
                     Missouri / St. louis

I find that no matter how bad the
Situation might be there is always a
Silver lining—even if that silver-lining is
that the Situation will be a good Story.
        Erin . . St louis MO.

8/30/16

The biggest obstacle we all face is ourselves. But knowing this doesn't always help at first. But we must keep working at it.

JASON 2016

I am finally free after 22½ years it is scary sometimes. But I am making it

Not everyday that rains is bad.... or something profound like that.
— RYAN MICHAEL......
CHICAGO

8/31/16

First name :- Dilip.

I'm sure travelling around is pretty important in anybody's life. The same with me. This mode of transportation is next level. Its economical, safe and coolest thing ever happend in my transportation.

Never judge sombody by its looks, don't know what's in there.

EVERY DAY IS A BLESSING! IT IS UP TO YOU TO DETERMINE HOW BLESSED YOU ARE EACH DAY. I'M A BIG SPORTS FAN AND ONE QUOTE ALWAYS RESONATES FOR ME... "IF YOU ~~CAN~~ LAUGH, YOU THINK AND YOU CRY, THATS A GOOD DAY, IF YOU DO THAT 7 DAYS A WEEK, IT IS SOMETHING SPECIAL" -JIM VALVANO THIS IS THE CHALLENGE I TAKE INTO EACH DAY AND GOD WILLING MY CHILDREN WILL DO THE SAME THINGS!

BRENT A.
CAPE GIRARDEAU, MO

Samantha - Tampa   9/10/16

~~[illegible scribbled-out text]~~

I started working at a
strip club as a server. You realize
that we all have our own grind,
own way of making ends meet. That
no one is better than you and you
arent any better than anyone. That's
humbling enough to change your life forever.

Alex → St. Louis, MO
The morality of people is a safety net
in the world we live in today. With all
the war, pain + suffering in the world, always
remember the good + morality within people.
That's one thing that will never go away.

Nich - St. Louis, MO
Life's too short to not have some fun along
the way.

Erin St. Louis, MO
A great time in my life is starting
nursing school. I want to tell people
to follow their dreams!

Always tell those that you love how much you care about them. You never know when it'll be the last time you see them. Music has been a huge inspiration in getting me past tough times and mourning.

— Sabrina, Chicago

Anthony → St. Lois   9/10/16

   Being given the opportunity to have a great
education and it's gonna hopefully provide me with
a future that i like.

Peggy & Shane — St. Louis

9/10/16   296 days ago I met my best friend
           When I see him my heart stops.
           I love you Shane! ♡
                              Peggy

SHE's tHE BESt ↑
              Shane

GOD BLESS AMERICA ( )

treat others like you want to
be treated....
Don't be an ass Hole,
and don't be lazy!
   =Lindsey

Eckart

Shannon - 2016 Indiana, shagunn@indiana.edu
Best moment, sticking head out of boat
in ~~Venice~~ Italy, and feeling fresh air and
sea salt, so at peace.
Hannah - 2014 - engan, MN, hkjohnson114@ymail.com
Best moment of my life was a 34 day trip to
Europe.

Mackenzie

I'm currently in nursing school and I
wouldn't be able to get through it if it weren't
for my mom. Hearing all she went through
to become a nurse has motivated me
to work that much harder in school to
become the best nurse + person I can be.
I want to not only want to make her
proud of me but I want my pt's and
all the patients I treat to see the love
of God through me.
Do everything as if unto the Lord.
I want all the people I come into contact
with to feel the power of healing.
My mom has showed me how to not only
become a great ~~person~~ but a great person
and I'm excited to share it with
those I come in heal.

You only YOLO once. Think
about it. If not now then
when? 2069?

- Trump '16

Drink Vodka. Be Happy.

- Dw
    - FANbuy - w How - mopw
    - Gpuw - ForGove

9/12/16   Dee from Missouri
   One good thing that has happened was I got 100 on my
calc test. Something bad that happened was I didn't
get ~~my~~ 100 on my AP Psych Test.

9/14/16   Michael – St. Louis
   The biggest motivators or inspirations
are people that say "you can." Most of us
are waiting for someone to give us
permission to pursue our dreams — Its a lie —
you don't need permission, but you should be
a person that gives permission even
though its not needed — tell people they
"CAN." Sometimes somebody just needs
someone to believe in them.

Tony, Phoenix, AZ

What has inspired me?
My family always inspires me. I want to do
well for them. As an immigrant in this great
country, I want to give them all the opportunities
that I never had.

St. Louis, MO
Resiliency.

GORDON - TERRA FIRMA

SPACE SHIPS AND TRAVEL TO THE
STARS ARE INSPIRATIONAL

9/15/16

"I never want to hear
the phrase - I should
have" A quote from a
- Captain of one of
the boats that
was part of the
rescue of those
trapped in NY City
on 9/11.
- Doug - St. Louis, Mo

"Imagination is more important than Knowledge"
A. Einstein (Gary from High Springs FL) 443 735 7757

in ferior
"Never let anyone treat you as an ~~inferior~~,
                                    woman   made
As a queer ~~woman~~ of color, I ~~made~~
~~in good company~~ my own place at the
table. Let Resciliency and empowerment
be your guide"
                              - Debbie
                              Rockledge, FL

293

9/16/16

live your life like every day is a
gift! because you never know when
the end will come. be kind to
everyone and help others.   Jane Sthon

"Absolutely No Regrets"
    - Talia, Minneseta

9/17/16

Someone once told me to live life to the fullest
and to learn something new everyday. make someone
smile, be nice as much as possible, never regret
anything... not even the mistakes, One Love

                              - Amber, South Holland, IL
                                Speech Therapist,
                                Student at SLU

9/20/16 There's a line from a movie
where Tom Hanks says "You never
know what will transpire to get
you home." Life has a funny
way of taking care of things. So
stay cool and finish your ribs
                    Best,
                    Joe + Matt + Kate
                    MN   ME   CT

294

9/17/16

Travel the world. Never regret anything
Bradley STL

Always be willing to accept a stranger as
a friend   - Caleb Washington DC

LIFE is short. Live everyday to the
fullest. Smile it doesn't cost anything.
Think Different... that thought worked
out pretty good for a small little company
called APPLE!! M Rahm
          Louisville & Dallas

Pain isn't a struggle. Pain isn't the end. Pain isn't
defeat. Pain is a drive. No matter what type of
pain you endure, you always learn something. From
touching a heating iron to losing a loved one, lessons can
be learned. But one thing that pain brings that hampers
everyone is FEAR!! Fear can paralyze a person mentally,
physically, emotionally, and socially. Fear can destroy
dreams. But fear can be defeated by... HOPE!! Hope
brings dreams to life. Hope can make a disabled person
walk again. Hope gives PURPOSE!!! No matter how scared
or how much fear someone has, it can never defeat PURPOSE!!!
Once someone has full purpose in life, there's no stopping them.
Find your purpose in life!! Because your purpose can
inspire others to find theirs.

          - Thomas   Chicago,
                              IL 295

9/17/16
Going → Wash U and experiencing
St Louis

                                    – Kumar
                                      Boston, MA

Experiencing true beauty; performing at the
Het Royal Concertgebouw.

                                    – Ryan
                                      St. Louis

Explore everything, search for anything, and
go everywhere until you find your passions.
Then, never ~~there~~ let it go.

                                A. Shah,
                                Chicago

9/17/16   Fred

My mom for being Louang
and showing me how
to be who I am today

ALL THE GODS, ALL THE HEAVENS, ALL THE HELLS ARE
WITHIN YOU. LIVE EVERY DAY LIKE IT IS YOUR LAST.
ANYTHING IN LIFE WORTH DOING IS WORTH OVERDOING.
                    BRYAN E. HOUSTON

Life is short + time is something you can never
get back. Cherish everything + appreciate
those around you. Surround yourself with
people who encourage, inspire + challenge you.
Always remember there is a higher power
above you. Don't take anything or
anyone for granted. Remain positive +
remember you are the only one in
control of your life. Geaux Tigers!

                    Ashley L.
-Louisiana girl living in Texas

297

Positive impact - Probably our summer family vacations to Table Rock Lake. We'd stay in a remote cabin, no T.V., computers or modern emenities. Great time to spend sp with our children. Long days on the lake, plenty of sunshine, laughter and good conversation.

Glenda Columbus, Oh

My 28 year old daughter is a recovering alcoholic. On August 26, 2016, she celebrated 1000 days of sobriety. ~~Before sober She is~~ Today, she is healthy, happy and the epidemy of strength. She took up yoga instructions and now leads classes for a ~~re~~ drug/ alcohol recovery program in Reno NV. She is an inspiration and encouragement to so many others who have tried overcoming addictions. I've never been more proud of any of her other accomplishments as I am about her recovery. I'll fly out to Reno on Wednesday to see her - and to meet her fiance'.

God has always been a positive influence in my life. He made me patient when I wanted desperately to find a wife. I had to wait until I was 30, but it has been the best part of my life

Andy
Vicksburg, MS

In 2013 I lived and worked in Kolkata India for 4.5 months. This experience fore ver changed my life and allowed me to see how lucky and blessed my life has been.

Kevin

Chicago

I work with patients with diabetes. Today I saved someone's life. They would have died in a few weeks. I feel good about what I did today.

—Mike,
St louis.

9/20/16

You make your life what you want it. Trust the journey, Trust in God's path for you. Never give up. One thing you must always be is a FIGHTER for yourself, and for your life, and through anything life throws at you. Two years ago, I pulled my infiniti over on the side of the road, on a highway up 40-50 feet in a city I was alone in and moved to for a man who ended up abusing me, cheating on me, and breaking my spirit. I almost jumped, after a bad beating one day. I cried and felt I had nothing to live for. My life became this dark place. I knew in that moment I was going to end the pain and something that day pulled me back. I left that man that day & never turned back. My →

300

life since has been nothing
But Blessed + amazing since.
God will Bring us to our
knees in the darkest
moments to Remind us
to pray. He is here, every
step of the way.
NEVER GIVE UP.

- Cristina,
  Clearwater,
  FLORIDA

Women have been a positive and
encouraging influence on my life. From
my mother, wife, daughter, co-workers,
and friends. They have taken me to
places and positions I never had the
courage to dream about. Their vision
and belief in my talents consistently
inspire me to be a better person and
lead a fuller and happier life!

Jeff
St Louis, MO

Money motivates me. Because I think if I got enough money, then I can have time to think what is the real important thing in my life. What's more, I think money is a sigh of success, I want to success, but why, I don't know. I just I want it.

Haoming
China.

My choice of a real estate career!

Beth
St Louis, MO

9/22

My parents have always inspired me to find what makes me happy in life. I come from a loving home where my parents have dedicated their lives to making mine the best it can be. I look to them and want the life full of love that they have built. I hope to someday build that life for my family and children.
— Julie, Chicago

Coworkers who are supportive & are like family. We spend more time together than family. I love my job & this family.

— Sacramento, CA

9/27/16

There is nothing as important as family. I've lived near family as well as far, far away. Although friends can fill in when you're away, no one knows us as well or is as forgiving of our quirks as family. They are the glue that holds us together and the inspiration that keeps us most human.

Rhonda
St. Louis, Mo

7/22 Sam, Scarsdale, NY

How I met the girl I'm going out
to dinner with, currently, is a strange
one. "OMG, you're Sam Fried! I
Know you through your ex girl Arlene
Morgan!" She screamed in the
loud and noisy club around 1:30 Am.

Jessica ___ - Kirkwood, MO
     I am an introvert. I love being
with people, but need time to
myself as well. My daughter is
2. She is a total extrovert. She
loves people - whether she knows you
or not she will talk to you. She
smiles at everyone and loves giving
hugs. In her 2 years of living
she has brought me out of my
shell. She is a wonderful blessing
and has taught me to love life
and make friends from everyone.

Chris Kirkwood, MO

- If you want to be successful in life you
need to step outside of your comfort zone

9/23/16

BRIAN, FROM WEBSTER GROVES, MO
NOW LIVE IN OAKLAND, CA
COME BACK TO ST LOUIS OFTEN, LOVE
MY HOME TOWN. POSITIVE FORCE IN MY
LIFE = I WOULD NOT GET TO WHERE
I AM IN LIFE WITHOUT THE SUPPORT,
ENCOURAGEMENT AND GENEROSITY OF
OTHERS... FAMILY, FRIENDS, COLLEAGUES
AND STRANGERS! THAT'S MY MAIN
LIFE LESSON!
~B

9/23 Jonathan Wichita, KS
I Value self-reflection.
Comparing myself today to
myself from a day, week,
year ago and making sure I'm
doing something today to
improve myself.

9/23 Nicky   Roscoe, IL
Of utmost importance to me are
my relationships with other people. I love
hearing stories + connecting with a diverse
group of people. I lean on these relationships
with others when I'm lonely, sad, or just
need a pick me up. Listen to others!

10/7 Jennifer - Chesterfield, MO
∘ Meeting great people!
∘ The goodness of America is still alive.
∘ Greater/deeper issue w/ America does
   exist
∘ Finding out who my friends really are.
∘ So grateful / blessed!

James,   Reading, PA

The most positive thing that has happened to me is overcoming my obesity. As a child I was 40 pounds over weight, and I went through a darm period because of it. But I eventually was able to save myself, my confidence, and my happiness, by losing these 40 pounds.

Jonah   Los Angeles.

The most positive thing that has happened to me was winning my league golf tournament. It took 2 years of failure to finally reach my goal.

Jack +   Lexington KY

When I was 16 my best friend died. But because of this tragedy I became a christian and was able to turn my life around and went from an alcoholic to a student at one of the top universities in the nation

Becca   Boston, MA

My parents have been the most positive force in my life. Both of my parents worked to put me through school, and they have made more sacrafices than I can even count for my well being. Even as a young child, my dad would ~~just~~ work on stretching my foot because it was born inverted. Doctors said it would be like that for the rest of my life, but my dad didn't give up & now I walk fine :-) Perserverance!

Abbey   Ann Arbor, MI

One of the most positive forces I have ever experienced was my job at a publication in New York city this past summer. Thank you to my bosses for empowering me, for making me feel confident, valued, loved, appreciated, important. I've never met a sweeter group of people ♡

Wainright Building
- Greg
   . I am architecture major in graduate school
here in Architecture. Manhattan — myself. I am here
by myself experiencing a city I know nothing about.
Washington University is the 10th best school in
the country & I've made it by myself this
far. I am my own motivation.

Steve E   Boston, MA

- You are the average of the 5 people you
   affiliate yourself most with. Surround yourself
   with people you aspire to be and, even if
   its painful, move away from people holding
   you back from achieving your goals

310

Kylie, from Los Angeles
A positive force in my life are
the people in the backseat behind me-
former coworkers who I met when driving
the Oscar Mayer Wienermobile. My
fellow Hotdoggers are some of the smartest,
most positive & motivated people I've ever
met. Though a Hotdog is what brought
us together, these are people in my life I
want a part of my life forever! y

Miss KB
You meet all of these ppl in
your life, they come and they go,
or some of them stick. Its strange
the things you can be influenced by,
Sometimes its a familiar face that
you cant quite remember, but for me
its the students life that I can
make the difference in. Maybe they'll
remember the lessons taught, or they'll
know someone cares for just a
moment. Lessons can be learned from
wherever you are, just open your
eyes theres so much to see.

311

Do you ever wish you could go
back in time? I do, thats why
you gotta live it up. Make this
moment count.
     Yes. I belive that we
should be able to correct the
mistakes in life. Even if
we could correct a mistake.
                    Nathan_STL

MY DAD IS MY ROLE MODEL AND ONE OF MY BEST
FRIENDS. HE TOLD ME WHEN I WAS YOUNG TO
LIVE LIFE WITH NO REGRETS AND ONE OF THE
PROUDEST ACCOMPLISHMENTS OF MY LIFE IS THAT I'M
THRILLED TO SAY THAT I'VE NEVER HAD A REGRET
IN MY LIFE AND COULD NOT BE HAPPIER WITH
THE RESULTS THAT HAVE COME FROM THE DECISIONS
I'VE MADE!
                    - ANDY - STL

My uncle comutted suicide when I was 12.
Never take those you love for granted.
Tell them how you feel and appreciate them.
You will find Blessings if you take time to
Look.   - Joe STL

STL is always thought of as the murder capitol
of the midwest, which overshadows the
the great people here. Uberbrings it out Tom.

Jesus Christ is our positive focus. We believe He is the answer! He died for our salvation and love Him more than life. We believe He died for our sins and to spend an eternity with us.

God Bless!

Andrea &
Tyler
Will

Tonight was my husband's
sister's wedding. It was fantastic.
Everyone had a great time! Brian
& Megan's father danced to "Who Let
the Dogs Out" which was ~~really~~ amazing
~~the~~ Sarah also made sure the Lego
song was played because everything is awesome, everything is
cool when you are part of a
team! Happy Wedding Megan &
Tyler! Now we are going
home.

Jacob,

Moved to St Louis from Kentucky for a job and a girlfriend. My grandfather had lived here for years so I had visited multiple times and fell in love with the city and its friendly people. I am from a small town in Kentucky and when I came here I was worried about the friendliness and hometown feel. However, St. Louis has made me feel more at home than ever. I hope that this continues for generation and St. Louis becomes a city that everyone feels safe and enjoys.

always leave the house cleaner than when you arrived.
                    - babysitting tips from my mom
                         kelsey, Los Angeles, CA

My parents have been the biggest constant in my life. They have taught me what unconditional love is & have inspired me on a daily basis to work to be a better a person

~~~~~~~~~~

I once had a college professor who asked what we were going to be when we grew up (haha). I said I wanted to be President. Yup. Of the United States. She told me I should set my sights lower – maybe be an assistant to a professor. — As my life's ambition? No thanks. Look for me in 2028. If Hillary + Trump can do it, why cant I? :)

Never let anyone tell you to lower your ambitions. Aim for the moon – even if you miss, you'll be among the stars.

Stacey – Austin, TX

writing about William Stokes!
He had a very interesting history
in St Louis. He ultimately died for burg
his representation that he was involved
in the trial of George IV.

Girl St. Louis
Wea. at 7 at
Left Bank Books

9/26/16

I watched a play recently, ~~scribble~~
that delivered the message
(I believe) that ~~scribble~~
everyone in this world is doing
there best. I believe that seeing the
world this way allows us to be
far more understanding and
empathetic. Often times we are
let down by others, but if you
carry the mindset that everyone
is trying their best, just like you
are, it's easier to forgive. Your
best IS GOOD ENOUGH because
it's all you can do.
              — Annika, New York, NY

Life is short, so live in the moment!

Jance
Fresno, CA

We get worried about being pretty.
Instead, I wish we would ~~strike weuan~~
be pretty kind, pretty smart,
pretty ~~scurum~~ strong, pretty funny!

— Anokhi, Chicago IL

Don't say "I'm unlucky". YOU ARE LUCKY!
To be able to be born in this beautiful
world, to be able to become who you are.
There are always those who seem luckier
than you and always those who seem less
lucky — just remember you are.

— Peter, Shenzhen, China.

318

always have a goal that you constantly think about and strive to achieve —Jason Los Angeles

Coming from such a large and diverse city w/ such a mixed background (Persian + Jewish), I've been given the opportunity to learn about so many types of people and communities, having been exposed to concepts like fashion, technology, sports, and race relations. I want to use this experience in my business career — to both make money and benefit my community.
    — Daniel, Los Angeles

"I am everyday inspired by my moms perseverance and kindness."
    —Katie, CONNECTICUT

Do you ever feel, like a plastic bag, drifting through the wind, wanting to start again?
    —Katy, California

The edges we live on are those static shock
white ones
Where brains become silence
And the world fades to want, want, want
    —Elisabeth, New Jersey

319

9/28/16

Life is beautiful. We should try to do
the things as ~~best~~ as we can
without worrying to much for result
and perfectness. If we do best effort
definitely we will get good results
too.

Pushpendra, St. Louis.

9/29 "You'll be ready when you Ready!"
John L-Tomm

9/24/16 Matt B. from Springfield IL

OK- Stay with me for a minute...
The Hobbit - Book, not movie (!)
There a scene in the book where
Bilbo Baggins is forced to enter
the dragens lair - by himself.
Very Beautifully written scene. He
tells himself that he has to choose
whether to go forward or go back.
He tells himself that no one
expects him to have made it
this far and to go on would
be the bravest thing he could do.

My dear father passed away 8 years ago. His presence is still with me, I have seen him over and over again since he passed. Shooting stars, his favorite bird, a deer walking by when we were talking about his love for deer. He is always there.

Laura
St. Louis, MO

Oct 3rd

My Father spent the last 15 years of his life, bed ridden, due to cancer. He spent 27 years in th U.S Army, retired as ~~xxxxx~~ a Lt Colonel, and also retired Civil Service. A month after he retired, we disovered the cancer. He never was able to enjoy his retirement and before he passed, I asked if he could change anything, what would it be? His respone: Nothing. ~~I have~~ NO REGRETS. He loved his country and family that much, He lived his life in pure loyalty. The ultimate patriot and my hero!

Keith
Amarillo, TX

321

I'm a student here at Wash U, and I wouldn't be where I am without my parents. They support me in everything I do, and I couldn't be more thankful. My mom and I both have a movement disorder called Dystonia, which is similar to Parkinsons, and while that can be difficult, it has allowed me to see how supportive and loving my parents can be. I am forever grateful.

— Hayley
Woodbury, NY

I'm a therapist for kids with autism spectrum disorder. I'm inspired every day by their intelligence, determination, and ~~their~~ love for the world around them every day.

— Claire
St. Louis, MO

322

"Second place is only the first
loser."
Never settle for anything less
than the best
                    — James
                        Fresh Meadows, NY

The most interesting thing about
my life is that I appreciate
the opportunity to accept and
find ways to conquer my challenges
because as long as I have a
positive state of mind and health
I will live to fight in the next
round of life. Because there is
always something new!   Khaliq
                        Saint Louis, Mo

" Hold fast to dreams for
if dreams die life as
a broken-winged bird
that cannot fly" —langston

this help me stay motivated
                            —Abryon
and go after my dreams
                        STL, MO

My best friend is my biggest inspiration. He is the most considerate person I know and reminds me daily of what the person I could be. The world needs more Jeremy Naple's.

~~I have been ill for~~ WAS

I WAS ILL FOR 6 MONTHS, BUT DID
NOT GIVE UP. I AM NOW
ON THE ROAD TO
RECOVERY

The greatest joy comes from working hard and making the lives of other people as rich as they can be
    - Sarah   New York, New York

I'm 7'1" and deal with a lot of questions due to it and a lot of pictures but it has taught me patience & humility I get to meet plenty of new people and learn so many new things. It has its problems but more positives than negatives.
    Luka St. Louis

10/5/16

John – St. Louis MO

- Surrounding self and family with other people who are aspirational themselves. Not just in terms of financial success, but more so in desire to improve their communities and those around them.

Kaz – San Jose, CA
- Currently living in San Jose, CA. ~~from Japan~~ We moved to CA from Japan in 2013 with family of 4, and it has been a great experience. Weather is great and working with the entrepreneurs and brightest minds in the world has been enlighting experience for me.

Takashi – ~~#~~ San Jose, CA
- Living in USA as a second time, 1st time in N.Y. and CA, this time in CA for a total of 10 years. Always exciting to get to know people and learn different culture. ~~Sincere~~ Thanks,

325

10/6

"I come from an immagrant family. My Mother & her family came here from Zambia due to work my grandfather did. My grandfather was highly involved in government activities & politics in both Zambia & Mozambique. He was determind to expose as well as stop corrupt officials that were self-serving rather than helping citizens. Around the age of 12 my mother along with her siblings & my grandparents fled to America due to increasing political tension that would put my grandfather's life in danger. His story is amazing to say the least, & as a young person, it inspired me to always seak out truth."

— Fatima, St. Louis MO

This Cant be stressed enough.
Meditate meditate...meditate...
If you think its difficult, its
easy... Tell your monkey brain
to just breath. Breath in and
breath out. Thats all meditation
is. Before you Know it, you
are resolving the problems of
your life...

Roham
6/13/16

10/17/16
Always surround yourself with people
who are better than you.
        - Anonymously written by
        a nice gentleman headed to
        Chaminade College Preparatory
        School's 25th Reunion with
        Two of his best friends.

327

Every thing we do can be positive
with a smile, a goal and a dream.
I think changing lives and making
people feel better and happy is the
ultimate positive experience,
Paula, El Paso, Texas

I really to be at St. Louis, very nice
City!
Gloria — El Paso, Texas.

328

8/7/2016

I'm a homework mom here, and I can't drive cars by myself. so I love use a uber. thank a lot. and I hope you have a beautiful life. again. Thanks. !

Have a nice day.
- Anonymous, wife of
an account opened
by "Juan"

That's my first month in US.
Actually, language is still the biggest
problem for me, especially speaking.

However, US is a great and funny country.
the experience in America I guess would
be a impressed memory for me, for so many
interesting people and things.

For myself, in America, I finally find what I
am more ~~inthe~~ interested in, Architecture
is a so fasninated profession, but I guess
it is not so snitable to me,

No Name provided
I believe I heard
she is from a
town outside of
Tokyo, Japan

330

10/7

We were given the pleasure to be the last ride before Donald was writing the first edition. My husband and I have gone through a lot in our first two years of marriage. His family has experienced more heartbreak than a family should. Cancer has been a word that has become too common. Always remember to live everyday to the fullest and cherish all of the time you have with your family and friends. ~~~~~ Always remember whats really important.

— Amanda & Scott STL